MW01611366

LIVING WITH MY X

The true story of one man and a rogue chromosome

LIVING WITH MY X

The true story of
one man and
a rogue chromosome

STEPHEN MALHERBE

Published by Stephen Malherbe

PO Box 144, Edgemead, Cape Town, 7441, South Africa

Publication © Stephen Malherbe 2014
Text © Stephen Malherbe 2010

All rights reserved. No part of this publication may be reproduced,
stored in a retrieval system or transmitted, in any form or by any means,
electronic, mechanical, photocopying, recording or otherwise,
without the prior written permission of the copyright owner.

ISBN 978-0-620-61286-9

Printed and bound by Quikfox, B27 Platinum Junction
4 School Street, Milnerton 7441

* * *

First published by Zebra Press 2010

PUBLISHER: Marlene Fryer
MANAGING EDITOR: Ronel Richter-Herbert
COVER DESIGNER: Sean Robertson
TEXT DESIGNER: Monique Oberholzer
TYPESETTERS: Ilze van der Westhuizen and Monique Oberholzer

This book is for you, Mom. Thanks for always being there for me and never giving up hope in me and my cause.

Contents

Acknowledgements ix

Foreword by Dr Graham Ellis xi

PART ONE | Of milk teeth, brittle bones and very thick glasses

1 *The Force* 3

2 *The origin* 7

3 *Growing up* 17

4 *Fairview* 19

5 *Discovering the neighbourhood* 27

6 *Struggles and games* 35

7 *Bikes* 47

8 *Rhodes Park* 55

9 *Inklings* 61

10 *High school* 65

11 *Holidays* 73

12 *The best of times and the worst of times* 79

PART TWO | Of superheroes, small guys and beardlessness

13 *No smooth ride* 87

14 *The seventies* 95

15 *Military training* 103

16 *Apprenticeship* 117

17 *Close calls* 129

PART THREE | Of bones, stones and endings

18 *A marriage and a sperm count* 137

19 *Martial arts and fragile bones* 153

20 *Ignoring gut feelings* 165

21 *Living among robbers* 189

22 *Bones, stones and endings* 195
23 *Passport control* 211
24 *Findhorn* 225
25 *Purple and orange flashes* 233
26 *A stash of sweets* 241
27 *Lungs, milk teeth and life lessons* 249
28 *Ongoing symptoms* 255

Afterword 261
   What is Klinefelter's syndrome? 261
     From Christine 264
     From Tina 270
References 275

Firstly, I would like to thank Layla and Dawn – dear friends who built me a computer from scraps and loaded basic software so I could start typing. The computer has since died, but they got the ball rolling – leaving me with no excuse to procrastinate.

To Dr Louise Lindenberg – thank you for the title of the book, which is both intriguing and deceptive.

To Maire Fisher for putting me in touch with Christine Coates.

To Christine Coates – without her persistence, this book would not have exceeded fifty pages. I also owe you an apology, Christine, for the many times when you pushed my buttons and I reacted strongly – I *do* know that it was necessary.

To Zebra Press (an imprint of Random House Struik) for having enough faith in the manuscript to publish it.

To my sister Christine, who initially resisted adding her bit's worth but finally succumbed and told it like it is.

To Tina, my friend and girlfriend – for all the times that you put up with my emotional lows. I feel that this book could never have been completed without your patience and understanding. Thank you.

It's often easy to trace our physical characteristics back to one of our parents, or even beyond. Thus, 'She's got her father's nose, her grandmother's green eyes and, heaven forbid, her mother's bum!'

These genetic traits are manifestations of our genetic make-up. The traits we inherit determine our physical make-up and are the result of a random and, perhaps, chance mix that occurs at the moment the father and mother's genes meet in the miasma of fertilisation.

Sometimes things go wrong. Perhaps the swapping of genetic material does not occur as nature has intended. The normal human cell contains forty-six chromosomes; half are derived from the father's sperm cell and the other half from the mother's egg cell. Chromosomes consist of the long strings of DNA molecules arranged in sequences called genes. These genes not only determine our appearance, but also the hormonal and other rhythms of our biological lives. Thankfully, while we may look like our parents, we are not identical to them!

The twenty-third pair of chromosomes is known as the 'sex chromosome'. This pair distinguishes male from female. Females have two x chromosomes (xx), and males have an x and a y chromosome. Klinefelter's syndrome people have been dealt an extra x chromosome (xxy).

In this book Stephen describes the profound effects Klinefelter's syndrome had on his puberty, fertility, growth and development. He describes his journey through a turbulent life; a journey fraught with misunderstandings of his condition and littered with broken relationships. He seeks love and acceptance. In this, he is no different from the rest of us.

But what about personality and behaviour? How much can be ascribed to our genetic make-up (nature) and how much to our upbringing or environment (nurture)? This debate has raged for decades, with behaviourists and geneticists flinging examples of returning salmon, migrating birds and identical twins across ill-lit halls.

Currently there is a growing body of evidence that suggests that genes can affect behaviour, which may explain the character traits we inherit from our parents. In Stephen's case, I am left wondering. I have no doubt that Klinefelter, with its protean physical afflictions, may also directly affect personality. I also strongly suspect that growing up and living in an environment that does not understand this condition may have worse psychological or behavioural effects than the condition itself. Ignorance and misunderstanding may severely compound the problems of the person who has to live with the physical and psychological burden of an extra chromosome.

Stephen's book is a disarmingly honest and courageous step in bringing these problems to the fore.

Dr Graham Ellis
Specialist physician
Somerset West

Each human body contains twenty-three pairs of chromosomes in each cell of the body. Each cell contains genes that determine our features, our colouring and our sex. Women have two x chromosomes – one from each parent. Men have an x chromosome from their mother and a y chromosome from their father. Klinefelter individuals have an additional x chromosome – hence a total of forty-seven chromosomes.

PART ONE

Of milk teeth, brittle bones and
very thick glasses

1

The Force

The year is 1975, a hot and humid day in January – one of the
hottest months of the year. It is eighteen months prior to one
of the most significant events in the history of South Africa
– 16 June 1976, the Soweto riots, a bloody day in the history of
my country, and a day that changes everything. But for the
moment I am still locked into the system that determines that
I have to serve in the South African Defence Force.

Apartheid has South Africa in its grip, and every white male
over the age of sixteen, born and bred here, has to go off and
fight – be it in the army, navy or air force – for two years.
Should I choose not to go, the government can sentence me
to prison for the same period of time.

I am seventeen and about to start my compulsory military
training in the air force. It is a big day for me. I will now be
perceived to be a man, not a boy. It is an initiation that will
prove my manhood; something I've been at pains to prove for
years. I am very afraid. Fear: I feel as though I have been kicked
in the stomach. My thoughts are all a-jumble and I cannot
concentrate. I have no real idea of what to expect. I have only
hearsay about awful treatment – my brother and his friends
love to tell of the horrors of the army. I don't even know what
to expect of myself. We have all heard the propaganda: 'The
communists are coming south, they are going to take over South
Africa.' Every night the radio and television report endlessly

on the situation 'up north' or on how 'our boys' are dying on the border for their country. Will I be another statistic?

I wake up in the morning at six o'clock, sweating. Is it the heat of January or is it my nerves? Perhaps this is how it feels to be going off to war. My military training starts in a few hours. I never wanted this; I am crying inside, but of course I cannot show it to the world. Boys don't cry. My brother, Johnny, and a friend are taking me to Pretoria. I almost wish an accident or something horrific would just stop the day now.

I say goodbye to my mother and Christine, my sister. As I walk towards the car, I hear Springbok Radio playing from the lounge: a favourite song of the seventies, Procol Harum's 'A Whiter Shade of Pale'. My mom and Christine wave from the veranda. Mom is crying. I bite my lip to stop it trembling – this also stops the tears. I put on a brave face and tell them I'm going to be fine. Who am I trying to kid?

The trip to Pretoria takes forever. When we arrive at the military base, thousands of other men are already there. Actually we are all just boys, all pretending. Their faces mirror my confusion and terror – I am not alone.

My brother departs all too soon, leaving me to my fate. My last bit of hope fades. Shaking like a leaf and hoping nobody can see my fear, I approach a gate, only to be told that I am in the wrong place. Laughing loudly, two officers ask, '*Wat de fok doen jy hier? Hoekom is jy nie by die skool nie? Jy moet by die skool wees!*' ('What the fuck are you doing here? Why aren't you at school? You should be at school!')

And they are probably correct. I am all of five foot tall and weigh a mere ninety-four pounds (about forty-three kilograms). All the other blokes are giants. I look like one of their little brothers, a mascot for the army, the kid who never grew up. I think of Clark Kent, who was a scrawny runt before he stepped out of the phone booth. I wish I was wearing a Superman suit under my shirt. I know I will be bullied – should I kill myself now? I should have thought about this before, I should have made a plan. I know I am going to die.

2

The origin

Let me start at the beginning. From as far back as I can remember, I always felt I was different, although it took a long time before I could find out why. It is one reason why I undertook the journey of writing this book: to understand myself. Another is to tell my story so that I can hopefully help others.

Our family home was in Fairview, Johannesburg – a relatively poor area. As my mother was the only breadwinner for the most part, it was all my parents could afford. The Jeppe boys' schools – government schools based on the traditional public boys' schools of England – were close by. They had good reputations – for discipline, rugby and a fair education that would guarantee entrance to university or getting a good job. I went to Jeppe Prep and then on to Jeppe High. My parents believed in a good education.

My brother Johnny was five years older than me, and my sister Christine only eighteen months my senior. Another sister, Pamela, had died of polio at only nine months old, before I was born. Anyone who has buried their child will know my parents' devastation at this loss.

My father didn't work much due to medical reasons and he found it hard to keep a job. I didn't understand why until much later, but he seemed always to be at home, which he didn't seem to enjoy. It was hard for all of us, as he was unpredictable and moody. We kids feared him. However, my poor mother bore the brunt of his moodiness as well as the added burden of his unemployment. Apart from managing the home, she also kept two jobs going for most of the time to ensure that the family was housed and fed.

My father was of French Huguenot descent, as our surname indicates. He was the youngest of five siblings. My father had multiple personalities, though no one knew why. Some believed sunstroke was the cause; others traced the problem to the encephalitis he had contracted years earlier. He often complained of headaches, which he mentioned to my mother when they were courting. The role my father played in my life – slipping in and out of his different personalities – was devastating. However, his behaviour prepared me for the many ailments I would experience. Only now, as an older person, can I see that I lacked understanding of his troubles.

When Dad was well he was generally congenial, but he could have his off moments. He often joked around, but, depending on his mood, we never knew what form his joking would take – was it going to be funny or embarrassing? The uncertainty was worse when we had friends around, particularly new ones who didn't really know him. Very often his timing was inappropriate. He would tell 'below the belt' jokes or swear like a trooper (my mother says that I, too, went through a swearing period – 'bloody bastard' being one of my favourites – and, no doubt, I was aping him).

A friend of Christine's once left the room because my dad had said, 'No brunettes allowed here tonight.' Everybody who knew my dad roared with laughter, but she felt too discomfited to return. I don't think Dad was really aware of how he upset people.

Dad loved ballroom dancing; he'd even won a few championships and had been asked to represent South Africa. Unfortunately, he had refused to go on that particular occasion – maybe he was in one of his 'bad' moods that evening. Sadly, it was an opportunity missed. Dad also played the piano, the saxophone and the clarinet and dabbled with the organ, but, although we begged him to play, he seldom indulged us. My mom had bought the organ for herself, but her playing was not a patch on my dad's. He was also a Transvaal boxing champion.

It sounds like a strange mix, but that was my dad. He was such a complex man. Although I only ever saw three of his personalities, my mother said he had many more. The ones I saw were *the joker*, who would charm us with his wit; then there was *the timekeeper*, who continually asked everybody the time and then insisted on changing all the clocks, even though they were correct. This was also his prim-and-proper personality, when his manners were impeccable and he didn't swear. The personality I found most difficult to cope with, and liked the least, was the man who forgot his surroundings – *the amnesiac*. It was like a case of early senility.

Much later, probably in his mid-seventies, Dad began to reminisce about his cousin Corky, who had flown in the RAF during the Second World War. Dad always went on about the 'damned Germans', the 'bad Krauts'. The memory of his favourite cousin, to whom he had been very close, always upset him. Corky was gunned down by a German fighter pilot just two days before the war ended. Whenever Dad told the story, I understood his contempt for the Germans.

Dad did try to work, but these attempts would only last for a couple of months at a time and became more futile as he grew older. His 'mood changes' could last for up to six months at a time. And he was always tired – he needed to take a nap in the afternoons.

Work would usually start off well. Then, after about a month or two, his personality would change. He'd forget why he was at the workplace and what he was supposed to be doing there. The job would suddenly become totally foreign to him. Obviously, few employers were prepared to be understanding. Finally Dad found work in a shoe factory with people who had a similar condition to his. The job kept him occupied, but the wage was minimal.

My father was like the fourth child in our family. Did he feel himself to be a burden – the man of the house who was not capable of supporting his wife and three children? Yet he never helped with the cleaning or the cooking – was this typical of his generation? I think he just wasn't capable. There were screaming matches. My mom would shout, 'Get off your backside and help!' He would do so for a few minutes and then stop. Was this due to a lack of interest or simply a memory lapse? Then Mom would say, 'You are so lazy. Don't bother.'

Dad would gladly go back to his reading, which he loved. He went off to the library regularly. There were always Westerns lying around the house – Louis l'Amour and JT Edson. After the reprimand, and after reading for a while, he'd call, 'Would you like a cup of tea, dear?' Her standard reply: 'That would be wonderful, thank you.'

All would be forgiven. Mom would tell me, 'I feel ashamed that I shouted at Dad, that I lost my temper. I'm so sorry about my outburst.' But the next time would be no different.

We kids were kept on tenterhooks. We jumped at the shouting and at my father's quirks. We tried our best to keep the peace, so we were roped into doing the household chores, but, of course, like all children, we did our fair bit of whingeing.

My father often had to be hospitalised, sometimes for as many as ten days at a time. There the doctors would administer electric shocks to try to improve his condition. It is horrific what humans to do each other in the name of science. Yet we never heard my dad complain or bad-mouth anyone.

Some time after my birth, Dad saw a psychiatrist, who diagnosed him as manic-depressive (known today as bipolar). This was just another label to be pinned on him – I would eventually come to understand how he must have felt.

My mother was one of four children in a family of Irish descent. She spent her childhood and her teenage years in Lesotho, at the time the British colony of Basutoland. Her parents ran a general store on an outstation. All the children went to school in Zastron (in the then Orange Free State). After finishing school, Mom left for the big city of Pretoria to become a nurse. Although medicine, and particularly anatomy, was her passion, she completed only one year of her studies. It was just after the Second World War and Pretoria was, in her words, 'a hotbed of Afrikaans-speaking Nazi sympathisers with strong anti-English sentiments'. This, in addition to the fact that she was very homesick!

At the age of twenty, Mom fell hopelessly in love with Dad, a man fourteen years her senior. She found him a kind, gentle and caring man and, despite family and friends warning her of the age gap and his lack of prospects, she married him. They lived in Johannesburg for a while. Soon, however, a pattern started that was to determine the dynamic of their marriage. My father lost his job. My mother decided to find work, only to discover that she was pregnant with Johnny. As they could not afford the day-care costs in Johannesburg, they moved to Vereeniging, a town fifty kilometres to the south.

There, Mom got a job at the Standard Bank. She cycled to work, as buses were few and far between in Vereeniging. My dad, too, found work for a time, and they thought they were settled. But then Dad lost his job again. This time Mom and Dad had to move in with her mother and sister. Mom settled down to be a mother , although she worked part time whenever she could. Three years after Johnny's birth, Christine was born. Dad found work then, but once again didn't hold down the job for long. After I was born, we moved back to Johannesburg, where my mother started to work for Price Forbes, an insurance broker, on a full-time basis. She would be employed in their claims department until her retirement.

Mom went off to work early each morning after giving us breakfast and getting us off to school. She'd return home by bus in the late afternoon, to cook our supper. There wasn't much time for anything else, as she left within the hour to catch another bus to her evening job as a cashier at a cinema. She seldom returned home before 11 p.m., and by then she was exhausted.

This routine continued until I left school in 1974. Some time during our growing up, Agnes joined our household. She was a proud Zulu woman who had to take work as a domestic servant, there being no other real employment opportunities for black women. Black men worked as miners or in domestic jobs like gardening. Agnes became part of our family and blended in so well that we just took her for granted. She did all the housework, helped with the cooking and cared for the children. We later found out that she was descended from Zulu royalty. Agnes was just such a part of us that I sometimes forget the big role she played in helping raise us.

I treasured my mother. She and I would often sit around in the bit of spare time she had and talk for hours about everything. Although she was kind-hearted, my mom also had a hell of a temper. Once, when I was a teenager, I was noisily playing soccer with two friends in the yard, and she yelled, 'Why don't you kids go and play in the street?' We ignored her and continued playing until we broke one of the bedroom windows. Mom came storming out of the house, took off her shoe and smacked me on the head, while I put my hands up to try to defend myself. My friends found this quite funny – until my mother turned on *them*. They sped off!

When my mother lost her cool, she always blamed the Irish in her. The Irish got blamed for a lot of things. Maybe I can blame them too.

At forty-two, Mom was diagnosed with sugar diabetes. She also suffered with angina and high blood pressure, but she continued to eat her sweets, which she just loved. She never changed her diet.

'The doctors don't know what they're talking about,' she would scoff.

It was not easy growing up with my mother always at work. I seldom had her comfort when I grazed my knee, for example. As Christine, my sister, grew older, she filled the role of surrogate mother. 'You clung to me constantly,' she often reminds me.

In later years, even though we were all earning a living, Christine would often share out money in order to spoil us (she worked in foreign exchange at Standard Bank). She was always generous and giving. Christine was one of my best friends and offered advice on many subjects – from girlfriends and dating to my motorbike (not that she knew much about bikes!). She always gave the best advice and I felt that, through her, I had a direct link with God. Even though I am now a man of over fifty years of age, I still seek her approval on any major decisions I have to make.

Johnny, the firstborn, always came home with merit prizes at the end of the school year. He excelled at sports, with soccer being his favourite. From an early age, he played ball in the streets. I don't know why he never pursued the game on a professional level – perhaps he lacked confidence. He used to come home at all hours after the games. Soccer got him out of the house.

Many expectations were placed on Johnny as the eldest child, but I think he had to take second place once I, the baby of the family, arrived. I can remember my dad picking on him for no reason. If Dad was in one of his strange moods, he wouldn't sign Johnny's homework and would continually find fault with him. Christine once described our dad as 'smarmy and evil'. No wonder Johnny took refuge in soccer. He could escape the sadness of being rejected.

But I think Johnny resented me for not being Dad's punch-bag, as he was. I came to bear the brunt of his rebuffs as Johnny took out his frustrations on me – like Dad did on him. Johnny liked to hit me, and although he made it look brotherly and tjommie-like, it hurt. He liked to hit me on the back of the head and then walk away, smiling. If any of his friends were around, the punishment was harder. Sometimes his friends also had a go, knowing that I would not retaliate.

In my early teenage years, I aspired to be like Johnny. I, too, wanted to be a good sportsman, but I always struggled and took too long to grasp anything. Johnny was a natural. However, I managed to outdo him in one area: I was the first to learn to ride a bike. Johnny was cross about it and learnt very quickly after that.

As an adult, I can now see that his aggression towards me was his way of dealing with Dad's animosity. I was the reason for his rejection, *and* I probably sucked up to my father to get attention.

People have asked, 'If he wasn't your brother, would you be friends?' Sadly, the answer is no. We are not close. We're like chalk and cheese. There was a short period of our lives, when I was married to Marina and our respective wives were good friends, when the gap between the two of us narrowed.

I can't tell how much of who I am was influenced by my family and our circumstances and how much by my genetic make-up. It's the old question of nature versus nurture; but such was the family of the boy with the extra x.

Growing up

My mother kept a journal of her children's baby years, which I found after her death when I was clearing out her flat. She writes this about me: 'Everybody says that with his good looks he ought to be a girl.' She goes on to describe me as 'very sweet and quiet – hardly ever crying unless something is wrong'. Mom and I were close. I don't know if it was because I was the youngest or I was easy to handle or I was pretty – like a girl – and she missed Pamela. There is much I don't really understand about why things happened the way they did. It was just my life and I had to live it the way it came to me. Now, years later, with some insight into my condition and with some maturity, I can reflect on my environment at the time and the impact it must have had.

I loved bus rides. Because we didn't own a car, the bus was our only means of travelling to the city and back. I had to accompany my mother into town quite often. As a child, I suffered from chest ailments. At eighteen months, I caught what my mother thought was whooping cough. As my breathing became increasingly laboured, my poor mom must have been sick with worry. She would have remembered the loss of her little Pamela. Mom somehow had to get me to the hospital. It was no easy feat taking a gasping toddler on a bus across the city. The doctors at the hospital put me in an oxygen tent and diagnosed double pneumonia. I spent the next few days stabilising.

This was the first of many trips to the hospital on the bus. I had to be rushed in for bronchitis and other scares – the continual trouble with my chest and lungs. On one occasion my mother was more concerned than usual: the doctors believed I had tuberculosis, but fortunately it turned out to be a false alarm. I have chest problems to this day – colds and flu go straight to my chest. When a docter recently studied an X-ray taken of my chest, he noticed scarring similar to that of TB, and asked if I had ever had it.

When I was well, I loved taking trips with Mom; it was good having her to myself. Sometimes we'd go to the city to shop. I remember that, at first, when trams came down the middle of Eloff Street, the buses had to move to the side. Later on, the trams were replaced by electric buses that had two long poles extending from the roof that clipped onto an electric cable running down the road.

It was a special treat to accompany Mom to the centre of Johannesburg City on Saturday mornings. We went to the OK Bazaars, then the biggest store in Johannesburg, which sold everything from clothes to food to toys – lots of them. I remember going up to the toy department, on the fifth floor. Once, I got lost up there. I could sit inside the enormous fire-engine trucks and buses that were like tricycles, with pedals, and 'drive' them for ages. I begged my mom to buy me one for Christmas, but she said that she couldn't afford it. But it was worth a try! I always pushed my luck, but she never bought me one.

Mom and I would spend a couple of hours looking around the shop and then go off to the restaurant on the fourth floor. I remember my mother saying how expensive the meal was – she'd paid twenty-five cents. Can you imagine? After that we would head off to the bus terminus and wait for the bus to arrive.

Fairview

Back in those days, Fairview, east of the city of Johannesburg, was a middle- to lower-class suburb. As I mentioned, the one good thing about it was that it had one of the top primary schools – Jeppe. It was so close by – only two houses away – that we walked to school. There was no chance that we could sneak home early though, as we believed that, living so close by, there was a better chance of somebody seeing us if we tried to slip home early than if we'd lived miles away. So my siblings and I never tried to skip school.

Of course, we were eventually proved wrong. Some years later we moved to Kensington, a couple of kilometres away. When we sometimes skipped school, our absence would raise suspicions and the teacher would send school helpers to patrol past our house or they would phone our parents to ask where we were. Christine was once caught when she bunked.

Going into Grade 1 at the age of six began my difficult school career. On my first day of school I experienced fear, sweating, a burning stomach, butterflies. It was an entirely new experience. I was alone, even though my brother and sister were a few standards ahead of me. I had a sense of facing the enemy for the first time. Up until then I had had my mother (or sister) there for me; now I was on my own. I asked Mom why I needed to go to school, why I had to be there. She reassured me, saying that I needed to learn more about life. I was really confused about all this, but it passed when I saw the other kids at school, some of whom were just as scared as I was. Soon enough I got dressed in the mornings and went off willingly with Johnny and Christine and some of the neighbourhood kids. I bumbled through Grade 1 quite happily, in the unconscious haze of childhood.

The battle started in Grade 2. I was a shy, introverted child – I was happy to play on my own, with other kids around me, not really wishing to be included in their games. But I struggled with the work; I did not seem to be able to grasp anything. The words on the board had no meaning. The teachers decided that I was lazy and that I lacked the ability to concentrate. I could never understand how the other kids seemed to enjoy themselves. I didn't know what I was doing wrong, but was convinced I had to be doing something! Too late in the year, it was discovered that I needed glasses. I was a gawky kid, very small, and suddenly I had to wear enormous glasses – they were nearly as big as my face. One of my earliest memories is of wearing the glasses and watching my distorted feet walking on the pavement. They seemed larger than life and I walked with exaggerated steps so that one foot wouldn't trip up the other.

Teachers in those years did not pick up on learning problems quickly. There were many things with which I struggled, and I felt awkward a lot of the time. Not only was I much smaller than the rest of the class, but I found it hard to keep pace. Eventually the teachers said I was slow and decided that I needed to repeat the year to catch up on the work and grow in maturity. It was a humiliating year, repeating Grade 2. Kids can be cruel, and I was taunted for being stupid.

At home, after school, there was trouble too. Johnny continued to bully me. His friend Matt lived down the road. I didn't like him; he always picked on me, making funny remarks about me and smacking me around. And he rather fancied himself. He and Johnny seemed to enjoy teasing me.

There were other kids living on our street, but I didn't mix with them often, as they were mostly a bit older than me. I was very much a loner as a kid; I was skinny and small. I looked like a little nerd.

But eventually I found a friend. His name was Brett, but we'd play together only now and again, as his parents felt he and his brothers were too good for us. College Street, where we lived, had about twenty houses in it – ten on either side. In some ways it was like a small village; everybody knew everyone else's business. The neighbours knew the situation at our house and about my father's problems. Most people felt pity, but others couldn't be bothered. Brett's parents considered anybody who didn't work a low-life, whether they had a medical condition or not; they didn't want their boys hanging out with the likes of us.

Brett must have felt bad about this or not understood why his parents discouraged him from playing with me, as we continued to play together every so often. Because Johnny and his friend Matt had joined the Scouts and played soccer, I was often left alone. I was usually quite happy to play by myself; I was used to it.

Christine was more outgoing than I was. She had a black friend who lived opposite us in the servant's quarters, the daughter of the domestic worker who worked there. Her name was Dolly. In those days, to be seen playing with or talking to a black person was unusual. We could face humiliation from the neighbours or from the authorities, but we were innocent and oblivious to politics and enjoyed playing with Dolly. Christine also made friends with another girl, Mona. Mona had a sister, Vicki, and a brother, Mark. Vicki was a year older and Mark a year younger than me. Mark and I soon became very good friends. He was a lot more daring than me and often looked for trouble. He liked to throw stones at people who cycled down the road; he'd throw a stone and then we'd run off and jump over a neighbour's wall and hide, waiting for the cyclists to disappear. Luckily for us, we were never caught.

I was about nine years old when I developed funny feelings for Vicki. I really liked her and I think she liked me too. We were young and naive and nothing ever came of it – I suppose she was my first crush. I just didn't know what to do about anything, it seemed. I often wonder about those early years of my life. I suppose at nine years old I wasn't into girls, but the feelings wouldn't go away – the first signs of puppy love?

I just loved being in Vicki's company. Once we lay on the bed under the blanket and tried kissing each other. We'd kiss and then pull apart and laugh. We tried it a few times, thinking this was how adults did it. I had an attack of the butterflies every time I saw Vicki after that. Eventually she began to spend more time with Mona and Christine, and I went off to play with Mark.

I remember an incident at primary school that will stay with me for the rest of my life. I was in Grade 2. At the school entrance there was a fountain with a memorial plaque on its side. Inscribed on it was a list of names – the Jeppe Old Boys who had been killed in the First and Second World Wars. They had all attended Jeppe Prep. I was walking towards the monument one day when I saw three boys sticking broken twigs into the nozzle of the fountain until the water stopped coming out. I witnessed the whole incident, but before I could say anything, the boys ran away. I wasn't sure whether I should tell someone, or just wait it out. As I didn't want to be a snitch, I just went into assembly.

Assembly was held every morning in the hall, and we usually sat on the floor and waited for the headmaster to come in and take the stage. He would talk about the day's events for about half an hour and then the teachers would add their bits' worth.

On this particular morning, things proceeded differently. The headmaster looked stern and said that there had been an incident. Some boys had seen another boy jamming up the fountain. These boys could name the culprit. The headmaster said he would like the boy to come forward and admit to what he had done, but nobody said a word. The three culprits were sitting fairly close to me. I turned and looked at them as if to say that they needed to go and own up, but they just sat there and gave me a funny look.

The next thing the headmaster said he would give the boy ten seconds to reveal himself. Nobody moved. Then I heard him announcing a name – mine! I felt panic rising up in me and a cold sweat spread over me. 'What is he talking about?' I thought. He asked me to stand up and come to the stage. I tried to protest my innocence, but he was not interested. The humiliation of standing up in front of the entire school was huge. I thought my life would end there and then.

As I walked towards the stage, the headmaster dismissed the school from the hall. I stood there alone with him. I told the headmaster that I had witnessed the incident, but that I had not done the deed. But he just looked at me and said I would have to take the twigs out of the fountain and help the school's labourers fix it. He also said that he would not mention the incident to my parents. It is something that has stayed with me to this day. I have often wanted to go back to that school and clear my name, but I never have.

However, there were some things that made life worthwhile in those early days. The ice-cream van used to come round; we could hear the tune it played for miles. We often got mixed up, thinking that it was in our road when it was in the next; the sound seemed to carry, or maybe there weren't very many cars around then. The van was white, with 'Wall's Ice Cream' painted on its side. Eventually the ice-cream man would turn into our street and stop pretty much in the middle of the road, cut the engine and wait for all the kids to come over. The side of the van would open up for him to serve the ice cream. We could buy either individual ice creams or a 'brick'. Bricks of ice cream: a childhood dream! My favourite flavour was chocolate. Often, by the time the van got to us it had run out of chocolate; I would have to settle for vanilla. Ice cream back then seemed to taste so fresh.

Huge McPhail trucks delivered bags of coal to our houses – big red flatbed trucks with one or two men on them to offload the order. I was always so excited when the truck came down the road – I loved the smell of coal. I could smell it coming for miles. I can still remember that smell and I still love it. In those days we had coal stoves in the kitchen. Agnes would come in early to light the stove and boil a kettle of water for coffee or tea. We also had a coal-burning fireplace in the lounge. The older suburbs of Johannesburg had gas piped to the houses. After a while, my mom converted our stove to gas – it was cheaper than coal and, according to her, less messy.

One morning, when I was about twelve, I went through to the kitchen. My whole family was already up and sitting in the kitchen. They looked at me oddly when I walked in. I asked what was wrong.

'Can't you remember?' one of them asked.

'No,' I said, and was told that about an hour before I had walked into the kitchen, grabbed the poker and lifted the stove lid. I then calmly pulled my pyjama pants down and urinated into the stove. When I'd finished, I returned to the bedroom, got into bed and went back to sleep. I had no recollection of the incident, but we had a good laugh about it.

In the backyard of our house there was a large apricot tree. Johnny and I often tried to build a tree house, but the closest we got was laying down a couple of planks from one branch to the next. I used to dream of sleeping out there on my own so that I wouldn't have to share a room with my brother. Unfortunately this remained a dream; Johnny and I continued to share a bedroom. We did, however, get the most delicious apricots from that tree.

Small pleasures are part of every childhood. For example, I remember the milkman delivering our milk right to the front door. My mom would place a plastic coupon in an empty bottle and, in the morning, the dairyman would replace it with a full bottle. My siblings and I used to fight over the thick yellow cream that rose up to the top of the bottle. It was the best part of the milk. Milk tasted so good back then.

5

Discovering the neighbourhood

Around the corner from our house in College Street was the best fish-and-chips shop, the Little Beaver. Just walking past this shop, we could smell the fried fish: the aroma of batter and oil combined. When I had any extra pocket money I would go in there and buy a Coke, which cost five cents a bottle. Every time I walk past such a place nowadays I recall that aroma. Unfortunately fish-and-chips shops today just don't have the same smell.

When I had a penny or two extra I also used to buy sherbet from Little Beaver. It was one of my favourite treats, one of the best sweets at the time. I recall tasting that fizz in my mouth, a bit like jelly powder but much finer and slightly sweeter. I'd try keeping it in my mouth for as long as possible, holding on to the taste, savouring the moment and, at the last minute, swallowing. I loved sweets, and I didn't have to worry too much about my teeth rotting. My milk teeth, which had taken so long to appear, seemed reluctant to vacate my mouth to make way for permanent teeth. When all my friends and siblings had their adult teeth, I still had baby teeth. Mom would look at me, smiling, and say, 'Just as well they're taking so long to come. With all that sherbet you eat they'd just get holes in them and have to be filled.'

Just as well indeed, as Mom couldn't afford a dentist anyway.

Later on, when we moved to another suburb, we found another Little Beaver. The only difference: it was a vegetable shop that stocked a few additional items. But for the moment I had this Little Beaver.

The local cafés stocked my favourite magazine, *Tiger*, which featured football tales, detective stories and the odd cartoon. Other favourites were the small, A5 Second World War comics, which I collected. I'd go along to the swap-shop and try to collect all of them. Eventually I had about two hundred. I loved to hole up in my room and read my comics or sort them into piles. I bought the odd *Superman* comic too, but it had nothing on my war comics. Another one I loved was *Tintin*. The Tintin stories were wonderful – full of adventure and history. I spent hours reading them. I imagined myself being like Tintin, exploring the world and saving everybody. It's amusing, but even thirty years later, whenever I walk past a bookshop, I always stop to see if they sell *The Adventures of Tintin*.

There were good and funny times. Even though I looked a bit like Tintin, I began to make new friends in the neighbourhood. At school there was a group of three friends: Mark, Luis and Kenneth. Mark and I were already good friends at home, but he spent a lot of time with the other two at school. They lived in the more upmarket part of Kensington. I wanted to be part of their group; they had similar personalities to mine. I had to work hard at muscling myself into a group. I was the small, skinny guy and no one saw any advantage in being my friend. One day the school bully picked on Kenneth. Up went the fists but, before the first punch could be thrown, I stepped up to Kenneth and said I would fight on his behalf. What was I thinking? But it was too late to back down: Kenneth stepped aside and the bully faced me. He was at least a foot taller than I was. I threw a punch at his jaw, but I never came close.

Instead he punched me and I staggered backwards while trying to fend him off. I swung wildly, but my thin little arms just waved in the wind. I took one or two more hits to the head.

'Do you give up?' the bully asked.

'Yes,' I submitted.

That was the end of it. In those days, if you gave up, boys still honoured you for it. Today it is a different story. After that incident I was accepted into the group. The boys considered what I'd done a heroic deed. Afterwards I thought it was stupid, but boys will be boys.

Mom had a difficult time keeping three hungry and active kids clothed and fed. Dad was still unemployed and Mom was working night shifts to earn the extra money she needed as the only breadwinner, and she struggled. I must say, my mother never let any of us starve. Although we took her wholesome meals for granted, there were other things that a little boy couldn't really come to terms with. Sometimes I was left out of outings others could go on – like when I was in Standard 5 (now Grade 7) and we had a class trip to the Kruger National Park coming up.

Anybody who could afford it could go, but Mom just didn't have the money. She could hardly afford the school fees, let alone a trip like this, so I stayed behind with a few other pupils who, like me, couldn't afford to go. The fortunate ones were away for two weeks – the longest two weeks of my life. I had to attend school as normal, with the classroom virtually empty. The teacher hardly bothered with us; we were left to our own devices or had to do endless sums he'd written up on the board. The thought of the others having a great time, more than anything else, made me feel very sad.

My friends all got new clothes regularly, but I wore hand-me-downs. I got quite upset about it, but I had to accept the situation. We got hand-me-down bikes too, from aunts and uncles who were trying to help. It was hard seeing my friends on their new bicycles; they had some flashy ones, the latest version by Peugeot or Sun, the best bikes at the time. Eventually Mom managed to save enough money to buy Johnny and me new bikes from the local store, but they weren't by Raleigh or Peugeot. We had to settle for a good old Humber. They were like delivery men's bikes, but they were great in their own way – they were tough. We could ride them anywhere, unlike the fancy ones.

One Saturday afternoon on a beautiful summer's day, Mom was in the garden with her rose bushes. Mom loved her garden. She looked forward to the weekends, when she could spend time in the garden. Even though she hated spiders (this is obviously where my fear of them originates), she could not resist pruning and digging. Our garden was filled with rose bushes. How she loved roses – I think almost every plant was a rose bush.

Enter an eleven-year-old with no friends around (my neighbourhood buddies were all busy). I was dawdling around the garden, looking for trouble. Usually there was something around to mess with, to keep myself occupied, but not that day. My father had gone off to see his sister in Mayfair, two bus trips away. I looked around the garden. There, out of the corner of my eye, I saw the A-frame stepladder placed on its side, as if it had been blown over by the wind, but there was no wind on that day. My mother probably just found it easier to pick it up from that position. I walked around for a while while eyeing the ladder. I suddenly had an idea: 'I'll give the steel struts a good old karate chop and see if I can knock out the supports with my hand.' I wanted to see how quickly I could remove my hand before the ladder closed.

I knocked the supports of one side out and pulled my hand away quickly, feeling the wind as one side of the ladder came down with a thud. 'Well, that wasn't too shabby,' I thought. I was sure I could do the other side too. This was fun. I ran round to the other side. I was excited and a little nervous, 'But here goes,' I thought. I knocked out the next one. *Thunk* – the ladder closed.

That kept me amused for a few minutes – I was quite chuffed with myself, but it was time to find something else to do. I walked towards the pathway and suddenly I felt a numb sensation all over. The numbness changed to a warm, wet feeling right through the centre of my body. There was a slight pinch on a finger on my left hand, as though it had been caught in a door. It tingled. I looked down, and then I screamed. My hand was covered in blood.

My mother rushed over, and the panic in her face told me that something was seriously amiss. She scooped me up, carried me into the house (yes, I was still small enough at eleven for her to carry me) and ran straight for the bathroom.

Mom placed my hand in the basin under the running water, all the while soothing my ragged sobbing. Although she was assuring me that everything would be okay, she had a look on her face, once the blood had been washed off, that I will never forget. She had turned white with anguish. I looked down to see that the tip of my little finger had vanished.

Once again we ran into one of poverty's drawbacks – we still had no car. My mother called my aunt, who took forever to arrive. I didn't feel much pain; it was more of a numb feeling. I just wanted it to stop bleeding. Auntie Joan rushed us to the children's hospital, where the doctor in charge decided the injury was not too serious. After a nurse had dressed the wound, I was discharged.

Two days later, I noticed a thin red line going up my arm. Although my mother only had a small amount of medical knowledge, she recognised infection. Off to the hospital again: the end of the finger was septic. The smell on removal of the dressing will stay with me forever – rotting meat. The diagnosis? Amputation of the infected area. I duly submitted to general anaesthetic and the surgeon removed a small piece of my finger. But the infection was difficult to curb. It took a month, one of the longest periods I can remember spending in hospital. Every time my mom and dad left, their departure brought on bouts of crying. Despite regular jabs of morphine to alleviate the pain, my finger hurt.

All this time I was away from school, and I therefore couldn't write the final exams. The school report came: 'Stephen will have to repeat Standard 2.'

Eventually I got through Standard 2. Standard 3 seemed okay, and I thought perhaps my life was back on track. I soon made new friends. There were Mark and Luis, of course, but I also met Desmond in my class. All the boys lived in the same road. We were never bored; there were enough of us to make a full cricket or soccer team. In those days we played in the street. We would place a wooden tomato box in the middle of the road and use that as our wicket. All our fruit was delivered to us in boxes, and we could also pick up empty boxes at the local greengrocer, so we were never short of a supply. We had a makeshift bat, put together from a wooden crate, and resorted to using a tennis ball, which was quite cheap, instead of a proper cricket ball. If we had to replace the ball, it wasn't too dear. Everyone was given a chance to bat and bowl.

But the number of times that we didn't finish a game! Somebody would either hit the ball over a wall and we'd have to spend a couple of hours looking for it, or we'd knock out somebody's window. Then we would drop everything and run away. By the time we plucked up the courage to go back, our bat, ball and wickets would be gone – claimed by the owner of the broken window. We would wait for things to settle down and then begin again.

6

Struggles and games

I continued to struggle with many things in the classroom. My new glasses helped me to see the board, at least, but learning a new language was difficult. We all had to learn Afrikaans – the other official language of South Africa at the time. One of the most embarrassing moments for me was when I had to stand up in front of the class and talk about a subject. I hated it, but my worst was when I had to try to speak in Afrikaans. I'd fumble and stumble and could feel the warm sweat saturating me. I'd grow cold and then hot again. I'd watch the other kids get up and wing it as though they were on a stage – I swear they thought they were performing for the Oscars. How I wished I had that confidence, back then. And how often the end-of-period bell saved me!

Little did I know that one of the symptoms of my condition causes one to struggle with language. I found it difficult enough to express myself in my own language, let alone learn a second one! As each class finished, I knew that another day would come when I would have to stand up in front of the class and repeat the excruciating exercise of having to recite or read something. At home I would try to practise by standing in front of a mirror while observing myself. This didn't help much.

But, as I've said, my real struggle was trying to grasp Afrikaans. I just couldn't get the hang of it. My parents kept telling me how easy the language was, but I just never got it. When I tried to explain this to my mother, she said I would eventually master it, but I never did. The teachers, who considered me either lazy or stupid, would tell my mother, 'I can't have him holding up the class.' I learnt to wear the 'stupid cap' often. I couldn't wait for my school years to come to an end. Today I would love to go back and tell those idiot teachers a thing or two, but unfortunately it's too late for that now.

At the time, I wished I could have explained to my mother how I was struggling, but in those days most kids were too scared to talk to their parents. It created a dread far worse than any fear we had of the teachers or the headmaster.

We all had to participate in athletics at school. The school was divided into houses named after different birds: Hoopoe, Kiewietjie, Rooibekkie, Sakabula and Tintinkie. I was in Kiewietjie, but Kenneth was in Rooibekkie and Mark in Sakabula.

It was compulsory to compete in all the different types of events. The teachers watched us at trials and then picked teams. The best went into the flat races – the 100 yard or 200 yard sprint. Besides running, there were also hurdling and relay races. I was chosen for the relay team.

My most embarrassing moment came after the first three stages had been run. The runner who was to pass the baton to me was approaching fast, and I was very nervous as I held out my hand to take it. He reached me in first position, but I staggered and stumbled and was the last one away. Then I had to run and try to catch up. Run I did, but I ended up coming stone last. I had let the team down; up until I had taken over, our team had had a good chance of winning. It took months before I could look any of my teammates in the eye. Time heals, as they say, but one never forgets the shame of childhood mishaps.

At least there were some physical activities that I was good at and enjoyed. Unfortunately these were not deemed an important part of a boy's development, and were not valued at my school. I loved riding my bicycle to school, uphill the whole way. This little exercise would take a good half an hour. Regardless of whether it rained or was scorching hot, we always relied on trusty old two-wheels.

My school was very strict; in uniform, we had to keep our blazers on at all times, even when outside the school grounds. I even had to wear my blazer when I cycled to school! By the time I got to school, I was boiling. The saying 'as hot as blazes' could have been changed to 'as hot as blazers'! It was such a silly rule, given the hot South African climate. There were times – at assembly or official functions – when we weren't allowed to even unbutton our blazers. If one button was undone, we could get detention. The best thing at the end of the day was the feeling of absolute bliss as I sailed down the road in the wind, hardly pedalling, as it was all downhill.

One day Mark and I cycled all the way out to Jan Smuts Airport (now OR Tambo International Airport), about twenty kilometres away. There were no freeways in those days, just the one long main road. We never planned the trip; we just jumped on our bikes and rode off. When we got to the airport, we sat there for a couple of hours and watched the planes coming in to land or taking off. It was such fun that we did it a few more times. In those days, Jan Smuts was fairly small, and propeller-driven planes were common. By the afternoon, at around 2 p.m., we'd head off on the two-hour journey home again.

Playing marbles was a craze at school. At last I'd found something on the playground to be good at. We all played *arlies* (slang for marbles). There were the small, glass marbles, and then the bigger ones we called *ghoens*. Most of my friends and I had lots of the small ones made of many different colours. Some were valued more highly than others. The smoky grey ones had the highest value. We'd go off to school early and play before the bell rang. The stakes were quite high. I lured my victims to me by putting a big *ghoen* down; the other kids would try to throw their marbles at it. It was a little difficult because they had to take two big steps back and then throw.

Most often, the kids threw from a distance of one foot, but sometimes greed got the better of them and they would lean right over the line! The more they missed, the more determined they were to get the *ghoen*. They would often bicker about who should go first and, in the process, end up losing all their marbles. Eventually I would have a whole stash, so I didn't mind losing the *ghoen*. I was better at this aspect of the game than at throwing: I wasn't very accurate with the arm and my eyes weren't good.

Near our school was a local café where Mark and I went after school to buy sweets. I remember buying Wicks bubblegum for one cent. The best thing about Wicks was the taste: a mix of menthol, sugar and what seemed like plastic! It came in pieces much bigger than Chappies bubblegum, which was wrapped in multicoloured striped packaging. Chappies tasted sweeter though, and there was always a little quiz printed on the inside of the wrapper. Wicks bubblegum also had a lot of information on the wrappers, but it was more expensive: we could buy four Chappies for a cent. However, the best gum to blow bubbles with was Wicks.

We used to drink water straight from the local taps and didn't worry about catching any diseases. Only later did our parents warn us that there were germs on the taps. After that we would cup our hands under the tap to drink the water.

After school and on weekends we played a game called tok-tokkie. For this, we needed as many kids as possible – the more the merrier. Mark had taught us how to play it. Luis always joined us too. It worked like this: in the evening, after the sun had gone down, we each had to take a turn to sneak up to a house and knock on the front door. We'd then run away before the person could answer it. We'd watch from a distance for the person to open his door and look around to find that there was nobody there. Then we'd roll around laughing.

We played tok-tokkie until one of the neighbours wised up to us. One night my friends chose me to do the knocking. I remember gently pushing the gate open and checking to see that nobody was around. I knew that my friends were watching me, and I wasn't sure which was the bigger challenge – them watching me or me having to approach the front door. This house's pathway was unlit, so it was pretty dark. We'd always strike after most people had had dinner and were just settling down to listen to the radio or read the newspapers (there was no television in those days; it arrived in South Africa only in the mid-1970s).

On this occasion I walked up to the veranda, took a step forward and lifted my hand to knock. But the door suddenly opened and the momentum carried my body forward. I ended up flying into the hallway. Before I could do anything, the man picked up a walking stick and moved towards me, obviously intending to strike me. With my adrenalin pumping, I jumped up and made a dash for the door. The man swung the walking stick at me, but, luckily, missed. I managed to run outside and quickly scale the wall. I didn't even notice my friends on the other side. Looking back on the incident now, it seems amusing, but at the time I nearly crapped myself.

We also loved playing hide-and-seek in our road. There were enough of us for the game to take a couple of hours. We chose the person who would seek by playing Ching Chong Chow (Rock-Paper-Scissors), a game in which a bunched-up fist represented a rock, two fingers (index and forefinger) facing upwards stood for scissors, and an open hand was paper. Rock could break the scissors, scissors could cut the paper, and paper could cover rock. Normally the game was determined over three rounds, but in some cases, when we needed to make a decision quickly, we played sudden death.

The hide-and-seek game could go on for hours, depending on how long it took for us to find each other. Eventually, if the seeker couldn't find one of the players, he shouted that he was giving up, and everybody would come together to start the game again. One night I got tired of playing and decided that I would go and hide at home. The next day, when I saw Luis and Mark, they asked me where I had hidden, because nobody had been able to find me. I told them that it was my secret and that they would just have to wait until we played again to try to find me.

A similar game was cowboys and Indians. The cowboys would come looking for the Indians. As Indians, we used to hide so well. Some of our houses were back to back: Luis's and Mark's were, and Desmond's and Kenneth's. We often took a short cut over our neighbour's wall. On many occasions, instead of hiding, we would run up to the shops, buy a cold drink, sit there for a while and go back about an hour later. By the time we returned, the other kids had given up looking for us. We did this successfully for a couple of months until one of the neighbours saw us and told the opposition: we were bust, but it had been fun all the same.

We also played a newly invented game that I thought rather silly: swingball. It came out in time for Christmas and everybody had to get a set. We were probably the last family to do so. The game featured a ball attached to a central pole by a rope; the two players would take turns to bat the ball, which would arc on its rope round and round the pole between them. At first I found it great, but later I discovered that I would have to develop some serious muscles if I was to play against my sister's boyfriends. They hit the thing so hard that by the time I took a swing, the ball was nearly at the bottom of the pole. Once or twice they hit it so hard that the ball went flying off the rope.

We played a lot of table tennis too, which I was good at. My dad bought the table from a second-hand dealer, but it came without legs, so we had to set it up on two wooden boxes. Everybody in the neighbourhood came and played on our table, but they had to buy their own bats, as we only had four. We started a league. I saw many different personalities emerge from people over the years. Bats were often thrown at the wall in frustration. (The neighbourhood kids collected all the balls that were knocked over the wall.) The funniest thing was hearing the excuses that came out of the losers' mouths – 'I slipped! I wasn't ready!' I eventually went on to join a proper club and played league table tennis for Yeoville. Those were great years.

Takkies were the 'in' footwear then; we all wore them. They were made mostly of fabric – a sort of canvas – and had metal eyelet holes the size of a pen top, maybe to air them out. This was never very effective for me or my friends – we had to throw them away eventually, as they became so smelly. Takkies came in different styles. Ours were flat underneath. The cool ones had tyre-like treads. Others had ribbed edges. Initially they only came in white – we used these mainly for tennis or sports like basketball and netball. Later on they came out in bright colours like red and bright yellow, but we boys liked the black ones that went halfway up our ankles, and fitted our feet well. They cost a whole month's pocket money.

In those days I was earning fifty cents a week in pocket money and doing Bob-a-Jobs, such as mowing lawns and clipping neighbours' hedges, in order to save up for my takkies – I very badly wanted a black pair. I had to beg my mother for more money, but she was always short of it, and I was forced to find many inventive ways to earn extra pennies. I even sold some of my beloved comics to get those takkies. We could buy a lot then for a rand. Some of my friends earned more than I did – they were in the one- or two-rand league – but we all bought and wore our takkies until they stank and pretty much fell off our feet. By the time I started working and had to stand in takkies for eight hours, I found them hard on the feet.

On Sunday evenings, my father and I listened to Springbok Radio, a popular station with many and varied programmes. It was one of the few occasions we spent time together. His favourite programme was *Test the Team*. The questions they asked were very difficult. My father's general knowledge was quite sharp, but even he used to struggle. It wasn't like the quizzes today; the *Weakest Link* is Mickey Mouse by comparison.

I also listened to *The Creaking Door*, a mystery programme, after which I struggled to sleep. Anything that creaked would have me in a sweat. On Friday nights we never missed an episode of *Squad Cars*, a series about the crime in South Africa and how criminals were caught. The programme opened with a characteristic burst of suspenseful music with a voice-over saying, 'They prowl the empty streets at night, waiting. In fast cars … these are the men of Squad Cars.' The story's introduction would follow.

On Saturday mornings there was a comedy show, *The Pip Freedman Show*. Pip used to adapt his voice and talk about the goings-on around South Africa. My favourite was another guy on the show who would change his voice and phone up unsuspecting people. For instance, he would say he was from the local shops and complain about something. The poor victims would lose their cool, and then he would reveal that he was from Springbok Radio. A presenter named John Berks did something similar later, on Radio 702. Late on Saturday afternoons David Gresham hosted the *Top 10*, featuring all the bestselling records of the week. There were also well-known advertisements I've never forgotten, like the one for Chevrolet:

A man asks loudly, 'What is your favourite meal, South Africa?'

A group of people answers, 'BRAAIVLEIS!'

He asks, 'What's your favourite sport, South Africa?'

'RUGBY!'

'What's your favourite weather, South Africa?'

'SUNNY SKIES!'

'And your favourite car, South Africa?'

'CHEVROLET!'

They all sing together, 'We love braaivleis, rugby, sunny skies and Chevrolet.'

We join in with the chorus, 'Braaivleis, rugby, sunny skies and Chevrolet.' Every white South African used to hum along to it.

When I was about twelve, all the boys wanted to make a go-kart. We would compete to see who could make the best one and set a time limit. We'd go to the local café, grab some tomato boxes and some crate planks and start to build our go-karts. We would use Luis's dad's garage and make a right mess. Nails would stick out everywhere on the machine and we would pick up the odd splinter because we didn't plane the wood down.

Bearings served as wheels. They had small metal balls inside them and were about the size of an adult's hand. The go-kart was about six inches off the ground. A tomato box served as the seat; the problem was that only two of us could sit in it at a time. Later we discarded that design and used just a flat plank. That way more of us could fit onto it.

Around the corner from our street was one of the steepest hills in the neighbourhood. We'd pull the go-kart up to the top of the road and check for cars. It was all in the timing: we'd jump onto the go-kart and fly down the hill. Cars would come in the opposite direction, but this never bothered us – it was great living on the edge. Our speed was limited though, so it was only a matter of time before we decided to make a few adjustments to the go-kart.

It was time for an upgrade. Mark came up with the idea of

putting bicycle wheels on the back, leaving the bearings on the front. So we changed the original design, but the new problem was that it looked like a Dragster – the whole frame sloped downward. So we put pram wheels on the front and used tricycle wheels at the back. Now we were about two feet off the ground. It was great, and it went faster than ever before. We wondered how fast we could go down the famous hill, and although we were all up for testing the limit, we could not all fit on the go-kart at the same time. Two could go on at a time, but there were four of us, so we came to an agreement – we would have to take turns.

Walking up the hill took a good fifteen minutes. When we got to the top, we turned the kart around and checked for cars. Off went the first two: Luis and me. As we sped downhill, I felt us slow down. I looked behind me to see that the other two had jumped on as well! We looked like tobogganists. But the kart started to bend and buckle, and the next thing, the back wheels were rubbing up against Luis's ears. We were going too fast to stop, and the seat was getting lower and lower. The wheels continued rubbing against the side of Luis's head. As we got to the bottom of the hill, the go-kart broke in half; I don't know what would have happened to Luis if it hadn't. That was the end of it. Luis had a bit of tyre burn on the side of his head and he lost a few hairs, but luckily it was nothing serious.

Mark, Luis, Michael and I were good friends, but things changed when Mark's mother married a big shot. We always referred to him as Mr Colgate, as he was the managing director of that company. Mr Colgate treated us as inferior beings – beneath his class – so he forbade Mark and his sisters Vicki and Mona from seeing us. I missed Mark and was quite sad, as we'd known each other for quite a few years. I also missed Vicki, for although she played more with Christine, I'd always had feelings for her.

Eventually my family completely lost contact with them. When you're young, it is a lot easier to move on.

7

Bikes

In 1972, we moved from the place I had come to know as home in College Street, Fairview, to Clacton Road, Kensington – a more upmarket area. These were years that seamlessly blended into my unconscious as days of growing up ... more of the same: Mom trying to hold things together, Dad hanging around in one of his moods. I didn't need Mom's attention so much any more. Now I had to make new friends and get to know the new neighbourhood. It was a time of just being – the lazy, hazy days of summer and games and comics.

During this time my mother took in lodgers. Whether she'd bought the new house with this in mind, I don't know.

Luis lived in Kensington, and I was so pleased that I would now be living near him. I also made some new friends in the area, although it was quite difficult at first. By the time we moved into Clacton Road, Johnny had already made friends at school and some happened to be living nearby. Clacton Road was split in the middle by Marathon Road. Our house was in the middle of the street, number forty-five. It was a three-bedroomed house. The fair-sized lounge had a room leading off it. Others would have used it as a dining room, but my mother saw it as an opportunity to lodge a boarder. Unfortunately the house had only one bathroom and no separate toilet. We did have a backyard with grass, but we weren't allowed to pee out there!

Now that we lived nearer to Rhodes Park, Johnny had his friends close by. He and Christine were a lot more outgoing than me, and making friends was easy for them. But at least Luis now lived nearby – his house was diagonally across the road. This was a great bonus of moving to Kensington. When we were moving in, Luis ventured over to help us, and the rest of his family came out onto the veranda and watched.

Luis's parents came from Portugal; they had settled in South Africa as it was considered a place to make a good living. Luis was a bit younger than me, but that didn't matter. He was also quite a small guy, like me, with a thick bush of hair and big brown eyes. He introduced me to other boys in the neighbourhood. At that stage just making new friends was a plus.

It took us about a week to settle in. Luis introduced me to René, a stocky boy four years younger than me, with brownish hair. His mother worked at Standard Bank. He lived two houses away from us, on the right. Luis said that most of the other kids were okay, but that a couple of nasties lived in the next road.

'Best to avoid them,' he said.

Michael was a friend of René and Luis. He lived down the road, towards Bez Valley, and was the same age as me. For reasons I didn't understand, Michael took me under his wing. He stood up for me if the others teased me. At last I had good friends and someone on my side! 'It's going to be great,' I thought.

When I went to school, I made a point of trying to keep in contact with Michael. He kept looking out for me. He was a big guy, very well built, even at a young age. He and his older brother often pushed weights at the local gym. Of all my friends, Michael was probably the best-mannered guy. He protected me many times later too, when we were in our late teens. He was great like that. Michael was a standard above me at school, but after classes we met and played together.

Michael's father was Portuguese and his mother South African. They were very strict. Michael's father was a bully too, and I began to realise that Michael had a hard time of it at home. His father forced him to be manly and strong. If he went home with a black eye, his father would ask him how he'd got it. If he said, 'In a fight,' his father would punch him in the other eye and tell him that he was never to lose a fight; he had to win. I think his father's actions prompted Michael to stand up for me.

Later, after we had lived in the neighbourhood for about two years, a large Irish family, consisting of five brothers and two sisters, moved into our street. Johnny and one of the brothers became good friends through playing soccer together.

We were never short of entertainment; with so many kids, we could easily form our own rugby or soccer teams. In those early years, Michael, René, Luis and I started to venture down towards Bez Valley. It was a sort of no-go area, a bit rough, but Michael was always game.

'What is the worst thing that could happen to us?' he asked.

So we crossed the invisible line and wandered over to the new neighbourhood. All went well at first – nothing happened to us. But one day Luis and I went to Bez Valley on our own and ran into some kids from the area. We were outnumbered and were probably lucky to get away with a smack on the head, a punch on the arm and a warning not to go back there again. We rushed home.

As we got there, my brother asked, 'What happened?'

We told him, and he said, 'This is bullshit – who do these kids think they are? I am going to get Neville and we'll go down there and teach them a lesson.'

'Great,' I thought. For a change my brother was standing

up for me. I followed him into the bedroom and he told me to repeat the story to his friend, which I did.

As he was about to get up and go with Neville to give these other guys a hiding, he asked, 'How many of these guys are there?'

'Five,' I said.

'And how old do you think they are?'

'About the same age as us.'

He took a step towards the door and said, 'How big are they?'

'A little bit bigger than you,' I said.

With that he looked at Neville, and simultaneously they said, 'Nah! Maybe another time. We will let them off this time.'

'Who are they kidding?' I thought. After that I never again asked my brother for help.

Johnny and I shared a bedroom, which was awful, as he bullied or teased me constantly. Our age difference was too great for us to get on well. My parents could have let us each have a bedroom, but there were the lodgers ...

Our first lodgers were a couple who stayed only a few months until they married and moved on. As soon as they left, Johnny and I had major arguments about who deserved the room. Neither of us won, as Mom had decided that taking in lodgers was to be a permanent situation, and she had already placed an advertisement in the newspaper.

My brother, sister and I all hated having strangers living on the property. Although they had a separate entrance at the back of the house, their room was attached to the main house, and of course they came into the house to use the only bathroom. As paying tenants they were given first use of it. During the winter months, we often had to have cold baths because they had used all the hot water.

Then two men from overseas arrived – Peter from England and Martin from Ireland. They were the best of mates, both in their mid-twenties. Living with these two was a nightmare. We all liked Martin, but Peter was inconsiderate. He spent hours preening, never asking if anyone else wanted to use the bathroom. He also continually chatted up Christine. She was only about sixteen, quite unable to handle the situation and terribly embarrassed about it.

After a few months, Martin and Peter had a falling-out and Peter stormed out, never to be seen again. Not that any of us was sorry. Martin stayed for eight years and became part of the family. When he was at home, he shared meals at our table. Martin's BSA motorbike was his pride and joy. BSA motorbikes were – in the late 1960s and early 1970s – pretty much in the same league as the Triumph Bonneville and the Norton – English bikes. They were like monsters and had a very distinct roar, unlike the high-pitched scream of today's bikes. And they were very heavy on petrol. The BSA had a beautiful chrome exhaust, and the seat was so thick and round, you could ride all the way from Johannesburg to Durban without having a numb bum. I loved the feeling of sitting on the bike and feeling it become part of me.

We knew exactly when Martin would walk in the door – we could hear the characteristic sound of his bike from a distance, long before he arrived. Eventually Martin moved out and into his own place. Over the years, as we all grew up, we lost contact with him.

I loved Johannesburg when it rained in the afternoons. The

mornings were hot and calm and most beautiful. Then, like clockwork, we would see the massive purple clouds gather across the sky. A few rumbles, a flash of lightning. Suddenly the air would go cold and the raindrops would fall in huge plops on the ground. The smell of rain on hot tar was a bit like the smell of coal I remember as a young child. We'd watch the steam lift off the road as the rain hit it.

I made friends with other boys, mostly younger than me, in the area. At fifteen I was still small and nerdy – but I coped by enjoying the times I had with my friends outside school. We trailed or rode the streets as teenagers do. My friends and I all had different bicycles; some rode ordinary ones and others – those who were really cool – had a new bike called a Chopper. You were really 'with it' if you rode a Chopper.

My mom must have had to save up for it, but she bought me one for my birthday that year. It had three gears on the crossbar of the frame – a bit like an automatic car with the gear lever. My Chopper had a small wheel in the front and a bigger wheel at the back and high handlebars with a curve at the top. It looked like the bikes from the movie *Easy Rider*. The seat of my Chopper was long, thin and narrow and jolly uncomfortable, but the bike was the coolest thing around.

One day Luis and I decided to turn our two bikes into a tandem. Luis said, 'Let's take the front wheel off and connect it to the back wheel of another bike.' Great idea! We decided to start at a point at the top of the steep hill just before it entered Kensington; that way we would reduce the amount of pedalling required. Five of us climbed onto the bike – one on the handlebars, the other two sitting sideways on the crossbar, and the last two on the bike's seats. We moved slowly at first and then started to pick up speed. We were doing about thirty kilometres an hour when somebody said, 'Did we connect the brakes?'

Eyes looked questioningly in all directions as we realised that we had no brakes.

'No problem,' said one friend. 'I'll put my foot on top of the front wheel and stop us.' Stop us he did, but his foot ended up being graunched, partly in the spokes and partly by the fast-moving ground. We went flying in all directions and landed with a thud. We all lay there in hysterics – except the friend whose foot had been caught. He was jumping around in agony. Although we had cuts and bruises, no one was too badly injured. Looking back now, things could've turned out a lot more serious.

It wasn't all fun and games, though. Johnny continued to bully me and take his frustrations out on me. He allowed his friends free rein too. It was time to learn how to fight back. As kids, my friends and I loved to watch Bruce Lee movies. I have always been fascinated by the various forms of the martial arts. My favourite was Jeet Kune Do, which had been established by Bruce Lee. It encompassed a form of Wing Chun, fencing, boxing and Bruce Lee's own unique way of kicking, all combined into one art.

As there were no dojos in the area where we grew up, I went in search of something similar and found a style called Shukokai and a hall where I could train. At this particular school, the instructor, who had been a professional boxer, combined boxing and karate to form his own style. I needed to do something to protect myself from the likes of my brother and his friends, who often took pleasure in having a go at me, and boys at school, as

Michael wasn't always there to protect me. To them, in those days, it was probably quite innocent – a slap and a punch here or there was doing no harm. It was what boys did to each other. But to me it seemed more like subjugation and humiliation, pushing down my already low self-esteem. I was such a nerd to them.

But I was growing up. I had more skills; now I could at least defend myself. And my friends were cool. They all wore the high fashion of the sixties, and I wanted to wear cool clothes too. Although I tried to fit in, I was both skinny and much smaller than the other boys. My voice was squeaky and I looked immature, while all my friends were examining the fluff on their chins. Some were even shaving, whereas I had the complexion of a twelve-year-old girl. Naturally, I was self-conscious and very shy.

Despite struggling to find clothes that fit me, I wore bell-bottoms and other fashionable pants, purple shirts and fishnet ties – the latest fashions. My favourite was a pair of stovepipe denims; they fitted round my legs like Glad Wrap. Although my legs were extremely thin and I was still the shortest of all my friends – so much so that I must have looked ridiculous – it didn't stop me from wearing them!

8

Rhodes Park

Although I always felt essentially different, for most of my primary school years I lived obliviously – I did not know what, if anything, made me different. I just tried to fit in – I just got on with being a boy and playing with my friends.

It was great being young in Kensington. The best thing about the suburb was Rhodes Park. I loved the park because my friends and I could create a world of fun and fantasy there. I could be a normal boy away from the cruelties of the classroom and the embarrassing poverty of home. In Rhodes Park I could be a king. It was like having our own 'castle', and the years of being kings in our own castle felt like the happiest of my life.

Rhodes Park spread from Kensington to Bez Valley and contained two rugby fields, two soccer fields, six tennis courts, a bowling green and a swimming pool. Many local schools swam their galas there, and private events were held there too. In the centre of the park was a lovely lake, as well as smaller ponds. The most beautiful swans lived on the lake, and they nested on an island in the middle. Near the lake was a Victorian bandstand around which was an oval amphitheatre. On Sundays various orchestras played from lunchtime until sunset. People sat on the grass or on chairs to listen.

There were wonderful large trees in the park: oaks, maples and Norfolk pines. There were gardens of flowers and various shrubs. There was always something happening there. On Saturday afternoons the local soccer club, The Ramblers, often played football there. A baseball team, the Malvern Imps, also practised there, and wedding receptions were held at the park restaurant. I saw my first fashion show at that restaurant one Friday evening.

It was wonderful growing up with Rhodes Park so nearby – there was so much to do. Often I cycled around the lake or I'd meet Michael and Luis there. We loved to skim stones on the water and climb the trees around the lake.

Most of us were wary of swimming in the lake, though. We were not supposed to go into the water – the municipal pool was for swimming. Also, people told stories of big fish in the water, and somebody even claimed there was a baby crocodile in the lake! It was probably just an old scare story, but we didn't want to take that chance. Then some wise kid told us that there were piranha fish in the lake. We all said that that was a lot of bullshit, but Luis and I didn't dare to test our conviction!

Michael, however, did like to swim in the lake. Eventually he got us to go in, despite our fear. He loved to climb up the willow tree that hung over the water and then drop in. He did it so quickly that we thought he still had his clothes on, but he'd taken off his shirt and left it in a branch. We followed, afraid he'd call us sissies. Luis didn't really know how to swim, and was afraid, but I'd just drop my shirt and shorts and jump in. Often we had to run away from the guards and hide up in the shrubbery.

One of the most challenging things we'd try was to grab a willow-tree branch and swing right out over the lake without falling in. Every time we swung across the water, we had to confront the prospect of falling in. I was terrified, imagining all the fish concentrated in one small area. In fact, the many

56

ducks swimming on the lake's waters would have distracted them – if they'd been there in the first place!

Once, when playing, we discovered a bomb shelter near the lily ponds, well hidden among the bullrushes. We noticed some large grey metal doors on the slope of the bank. At first they looked like a couple of steel doors lying on the hillside, but as we got closer we saw that they were padlocked. We asked around and were told that the shelter could hold about twenty people and had been constructed during the Second World War, possibly to store ammunition or even a canon to protect Johannesburg from invasion by the Germans. Of course our young minds made up all kinds of stories.

Rhodes Park also had its own library, from which I got some of my best books. I have always been fascinated by shipwrecks and I found books about them. I also enjoyed crime and adventure stories. Then I discovered the library kept *Tintin* books, which I took out, as they were too expensive to purchase and I could read them as many times as I liked.

We swam in the municipal swimming pool too. During the holidays or on weekends I often spent the whole day there with Luis and Michael. We would swim for hours, but the big thing was to lie in the sun and try to get a tan. We never used sunscreen, or 'suntan lotion'; we'd never heard of it! We just lay in the sun trying to turn as brown as possible. The skin often peeled right off our bodies, but nobody wanted to be the first to get up. We didn't want to be called 'chicken', so we just lay there and baked. Often I could hardly walk home, I was so burnt and red, and I suffered badly when I took a bath.

All this would be forgotten later in the week when I had a golden-brown tan: so cool. Later Coppertone suntan oil came onto the market, which we started using. Its smell – a coconut-like fragrance – always reminds me of the advert for that famous brand: the bottle featured a naughty little dog pulling down a little girl's bikini briefs. Every time somebody mentions suntan lotion, that image comes to mind. If I remember correctly, the adverts for that lotion were banned in South Africa later on because the censors didn't like the little girl showing part of her bum.

As much as we loved to play in Rhodes Park, it was a drag to walk the mile home (in those days we still measured everything in miles); I was therefore glad I had a bike. Before I got it, my friends and I found it much easier to play in the street, as we'd only have to walk a couple of paces and we were home.

I loved walking our dog, Ringo, in Rhodes Park. Of course then I'd walk instead of ride over, with only Ringo for company. My favourite time was just after the gardeners had mowed the grass – I could hear the big industrial lawnmowers from our house. I loved the smell of freshly-cut grass (and still do) – it was like spring in the air, a sweet smell. I wanted to go to the park as soon as I heard the mowers so that I could go and roll in the grass. So every time they mowed the lawn, I would grab the dog's lead and run there to enjoy a couple of hours of inhaling the grass! I was quite happy to walk through the park on my own; I didn't need anybody with me.

One reason my friends and I went to Rhodes Park for adventures whenever we could was that it was a place filled with myth and danger. Besides the fascination of the bomb shelter, a legendary story of robbers captured our young minds. We had heard the tale from the grown-ups. The story went that, long before, at the beginning of the twentieth century, Kensington had been home to one of the most notorious gangs in Johannesburg, the Foster Gang, which hid in the surrounding hills and robbed banks.

In 1914, the Foster Gang was travelling from Cape Town to Johannesburg, robbing and murdering people along the way. The members of the gang were Carl Mezar, John Maxim – an American gunman on the run – and William Foster. They were accompanied by Foster's wife, Peggy. When they arrived in Johannesburg, they hid out in the Kensington hills, in a cave.

The police had set up roadblocks to catch the gang on Main Reef Road when a Dr Gerald Grace of Springs (the nephew of the cricketer WG Grace) came travelling down the road. The police indicated for him to stop, but he just drove on. They immediately opened fire, thinking it was the Foster Gang, and hit Dr Grace in the neck. His wife was hit in the arm, but would survive. Dr Grace was not so lucky.

On 15 September, on the other side of town – on Main Reef Road going west – there was another roadblock. General Koos de la Rey was travelling in a car with General Beyers, first commandant-general of the Union Defence Force. They, too, failed to stop and a constable knelt down in the road, took aim and fired. He missed the speeding car, but the bullet ricocheted off the road and passed clean through De la Rey's heart. It was a tragedy. General de la Rey was famous as a hero of the Anglo-Boer War; he had captured Lord Methuen, and, earlier, rounded up Jameson's private army.

Sniffer dogs eventually picked up the gang's scent at Bedford Farm and the police followed the trail to the cave. A shoot-out ensued. The police shouted for the gang to surrender, but William Foster said that he wanted to see his wife and baby, who had been staying with relatives in Germiston. The police sent for them, and when Foster's wife and her sister arrived, they went into the cave. The policemen waited outside, and a few minutes later the sister emerged with the baby. Moments later shots rang out in the cave and all went quiet. When the police entered the cave, they found all of the gang dead; suicide had been their only way out.

Many years later my karate instructor dug in the cave. By that time the cave, and the property it was on, belonged to a private owner, so he had to get permission for the dig. All he found was a few bottles, a bullet shell and a shoe.

9

Inklings

Life in the sixties was difficult for my family. My mother worked extremely hard, with my father still struggling to keep employment. Apartheid was in full force, and, as white people, we had a fairly good life compared to those of black people, who had a much harder time. Yet we struggled. Agnes, who had worked for us in Fairview, moved with us to Kensington. All in all she was with us for about thirty years. She was like a second mother to me, I suppose – a shadow mother whom I took for granted, for whenever I arrived home from school, she was there with lunch and tea. She washed and ironed our clothes and cleaned our house. My mother worked so hard at earning an income to keep us all going, yet, as I grew older, I didn't miss her too much because Agnes was always there to meet my needs.

As a kid, I could never understand why we were scolded by our neighbours for talking to black people. In the eyes of a child there is no difference between people, but, of course, in South Africa at that time, black people were classed as inferior. Most people around me called black people 'kaffirs'. You heard this everywhere.

I remember police vehicles patrolling the streets and the cops demanding black people's passbooks. I hated it when I saw Agnes being stopped and asked for hers. It happened to all the black people – they were not even allowed to walk around after nine o'clock at night.

Agnes was a very big, round woman, about the same age as my mother. She carried herself with great dignity. We were a little afraid of her! Yet the police could stop her in the street and speak to her as if she were a child. But I noticed that she never cowered when confronted, and soon the policeman would change his tone and speak to her with a little more respect. It's hard to imagine how it must have been for her to come from such a noble family and take a job as a domestic worker. We only found out that she was royalty from the friends who came to visit her. They would often say that Agnes was an important woman in her hometown, but we just brushed this aside.

When we moved to Kensington, Agnes opened a shebeen – an illegal liquor store and bar – at the back of our house. Shebeens were found mostly in the townships but, in some cases, in the backyards of white people's houses too. They sold mainly Black Label and Lion beer, but they also offered a home-made brew, sorghum beer (we knew it just as 'kaffir beer'). This beer was white and creamy, like white foam. It reminded me of milk stout, and was often kept in five-litre drums. Black people loved this traditional beer but, in the apartheid years, the sale of liquor was strictly controlled. Obtaining a liquor licence was very difficult – the police would often raid even pubs that were legal and demand to see their licences. The mere thought of a black person owning a bar was out of the question.

The police arrived at our house a few times, asking questions about Agnes and her shebeen. Amazingly, she always avoided being arrested. Later I realised that whenever the police were in the area, they called on the local shebeen and purchased a few drinks – it was a case of one hand washing the other.

In those days, if domestic workers lived on the premises of their employers, their husbands or boyfriends could not stay with them. Most of their husbands stayed in the 'homelands' – Zululand or the Transkei. It was terribly sad. I can't imagine having my loved one living so far away.

One good thing about having Agnes around was that she was feared by most people, men and women alike. Once, when we were in our teens, a man crawled up the front stairs onto the veranda and tried to sneak into our house. Agnes waited for him, iron in hand. As he was about to make off with some items, she didn't hesitate – she just hit him on the head a couple of times and then called the police. Word got out very quickly after that to any would-be thieves.

When we were kids growing up, there was constant talk of how the communists were coming, fighting their way down Africa. The government used people's fear of communism to frighten and control them. Those were the days of Nelson Mandela's trial and the beginnings of black resistance. Any person who went against the government was thought to be a communist.

One December, Agnes went home to Zululand, as she did every year. However, when January came, she didn't return. In those days, we had to rely on the neighbours' domestic workers for information, as there were no telephone links to the home-lands, but none of them had any information about Agnes. So we waited. About a month later, Agnes's sister Martha came from her home and told us Agnes would not be coming back.

She went on to tell us solemnly that Agnes had died. We were absolutely horrified. My mother burst into tears. She had known Agnes for so long – she had worked for us since Johnny was a baby. Martha asked if she could work in Agnes's place and my mother agreed, and so we tried to get on with our lives.

We desperately wanted to know more about the circumstances of Agnes's death, but Martha could tell us nothing more.

Agnes would only have been about fifty-five. She had been healthy and fit and too young to die. A few months later, we learnt the truth from one of her friends, Thomas, who lived down the road. Agnes had been a very important woman in her homeland, he told us. He said that, when her father died, Agnes would rule over her people. Agnes, he said, had been murdered; he thought her enemies had probably poisoned her. Months later, we heard this from other sources too. Then, many years on, I bumped into one of Agnes's friends, a man who had grown up with her family. He told me pretty much the same story.

One song that always reminds me of Agnes is 'A Swinging Safari' by Bert Kaempfert. I used to hear music coming from the radio in her room – the sounds of Soweto and the jazz sounds of America.

I remember when my mother and I walked down the street, a black person had to step off the pavement and let us pass if they were walking towards us. I asked my mother why this was, and she said that it was the law in South Africa. I was uncomfortable with this; it seemed so unfair, but I was just a child at the time.

Even though I, too, was sometimes treated unfairly, I didn't question the injustices of this country deeply enough. Instead, my preoccupations were with my own body. I'd begun to notice that Michael and Luis's bodies were changing. Mine was not: I stayed small and skinny while they grew taller and stronger. Michael grew a few inches that year, and Luis just shot up. Their bodies grew more muscular and they were much better at sports than I was.

10

High school

I started my senior education at Jeppe Boys' High, very much a typical boys' school. Participating in sport – especially rugby – was compulsory. We also all had to be in the cadets. The whole school ethos was to produce tough young men who were good at sport and could go on to serve in the military. It was all about muscles and marks.

We were expected to go to university, and the teachers pushed academic subjects like Latin, maths and science. There were some more practical subjects for boys who were not academically inclined, but clever boys had more status. Although this kind of school was modelled on English public schools, the government sponsored all the costs. Our competitors were other good boys' schools in Johannesburg – Parktown Boys', King Edwards – and schools further afield, such as Pretoria Boys' and Potch.

In winter we had to play rugby, since it was the equivalent of a state religion. Our dads listened to the radio commentaries on big games and sometimes went to watch matches at Ellis Park. I never went with my dad, but at school I knew I was expected to play rugby. How I hated it – more locker rooms and comparisons. I was still very small and scrawny and had a huge complex about the size of my genitals.

On weekends we had to attend the first- and second-team matches. I had better things to do on a Saturday afternoon, but the prefects watched our every move. They held a roll-call for every class and, boy, did we have to have a good reason not to attend – only our death might've been accepted as an excuse for not being there! The compulsory summer sports were cricket, tennis and athletics. I preferred softer sports like table tennis, as I was still very small and underdeveloped. I have never had much ball sense; I'd practise a great deal to get my eye in. Table tennis was about the only sport I seemed able to master, but I still wore glasses – thick, black-framed ones (contact lenses weren't available then). When I participated in any form of sport, my glasses jumped up and down on my face, and often fell off. So I fixed elastic bands to the arms and tied these around my head to keep the glasses on my face. This solution was not a good idea: I was always being ridiculed by my classmates.

I can remember the time when I first tried rugby. I retain this ridiculous image of myself running with a rugby ball under my arm, and half the team, who were twice my size, chasing after me and tackling me. Of course, my glasses fell off and I couldn't see a thing.

I was useless in the team and didn't find the game much fun. Whenever I tried to tackle one of the boys, I was like a little fly bothering him – the boys just swiped me off with a casual blow. I can still see myself hanging onto a player three times my size. After he'd dived across the line and scored a try, he looked around and smirked, 'Oh! Is that you, little fly, still hanging onto me?'

I never had confidence at the required sports at school. And I didn't really know I was good at other sports like table tennis or the martial arts, as they were not official school games and held no value at school. I was also troubled by a lack of self-esteem because I didn't have the physical strength required for the compulsory sports.

To survive and be admired in a boys' school system, I would have to have been one of the jocks – they seemed to enjoy the easy life. Deep inside I wanted so badly to participate. It would have been a big thing for me to be accepted into the 'clan'. However, my fellow pupils saw me as the wimp of the century.

Only once, I recall, was there a triumphant moment in my school days, in Standard 8. Our class – about fifteen of us – was busy with the task of cleaning up the gym when somebody found an old table-tennis table and a few bats lying around. We set it up. The strongest pushed themselves forward to play. I begged for a game, but the more dominant guys just laughed and said I would be no good.

Finally, one of them said, 'Okay, let's give Stephen a try. This will be a good laugh.'

I grasped the opportunity. They couldn't believe their eyes. I beat one of my opponents 21-0 – a whitewash. A kid who thought he was the hottest thing around – I think his name was Martin – challenged me. We started to play. Soon he started to make excuses for every shot he missed. I ended up beating him two games to one. I was a hero for a day. But soon my situation returned to normal.

One day, when I was messing around with a rugby ball, drop-kicking it over the posts, a teacher noticed me and suggested I play scrumhalf. He said I was a good kicker and that they needed somebody on the team. He told me to be at the next practice, but I never pitched up. I was just too scared; those guys were enormous. Of course, the teacher was angry and reported me to the head of rugby. I was called in and threatened with a disciplinary hearing. *All* boys had to play rugby.

'It will make a man out of you,' he said.

My mother sympathised with me. She must have known how vulnerable I was and she managed to get doctors' letters stating that I was not medically fit to play. I was relieved when the school accepted these excuses and I thus managed to get out of playing sports. After that, I never participated in any official sport at school, but of course that just made my life more difficult.

It was in the locker rooms at school or at the swimming pool that I really noticed things had changed. Boys stood in lines to wee, holding their penises and, of course, comparing sizes. On the sports fields they all outstripped me. They made the teams – rugby and cricket – and I sat on the bench. While I stayed on the outside of manhood, they all embraced it.

One day, as we were playing a game of cricket in the street outside our house, Judy, a girl from down the road, walked past. She stopped to watch the match for a while, focusing her gaze on Michael. Luis bowled and Michael was out. It was my turn. I stepped up to take the bat and she let out a hoot of laughter.

'Look at the shrimp!' she pointed and laughed. 'You're not going to let him bat, are you? He's no bigger than the bat itself!'

She howled with mirth and others joined her, all pointing at me. I put the bat down and turned away. But Michael protected me. He called me to return to the wicket.

'Shuddup!' he snarled at Judy. 'Leave him alone. You're too fat to play cricket, anyway!'

That took the smile off her face and she slunk away. Michael had no reason to protect me – he was an alpha male – but I will never forget the show of support. I needed as much as I could get. The trauma of the urinals continued and I often peed in the toilet pan with the door closed. I noticed with horror that my testes, too, were minute compared to those of the other boys. They were growing cocks and balls while mine remained the size of a young child. My smallness became my constant preoccupation. But this wasn't my only problem.

The boys had begun going out with girls. There were parties and party games: Kissing Touches and Spin the Bottle. The others seemed to love these games. The girls were silly and giggled and ran about screaming loudly, but mysteriously slowed down to be caught – by Michael in particular. Luis and René had to work a little harder, but they all caught girls. I never did, and it was not because I couldn't run. The girls never allowed me to catch them. When we played Spin the Bottle, they didn't have as much control. Inevitably the bottle would point to me and then I was humiliated all over again: the girls would squeal and avoid kissing me. I longed to be kissed, of course, but I had to pretend that I didn't care.

Playground talk had evolved from marbles and pets to wet dreams and first base. It was as if the others were all members of a secret club to which I could not belong. Michael really seemed to know what was what. He spoke as if he had vast experience with women, and as a result all the boys looked up to him. The girls swooned whenever he passed. Inexplicably, he still protected me. I was a runt who never built up a sweat when I exercised. I pretended to be interested in girls, but I was more into having a good time playing with my friends or going to the movies. Michael was the hero of the school and the playground and didn't need to be kind to me, but he was.

Our tastes for entertainment began to change too; we chose to go to the cinema – the 'bioscope', as our parents called it – more often than to go for a swim. I was relieved, as I was ever more self-conscious and did not want to bare myself in front of others.

On Saturday afternoons the local bioscope screened cowboy films. A ticket cost just fifteen cents and we pooled our pocket money to buy popcorn or sweets. Michael, Luis and I saw every John Wayne film that was shown. We loved *True Grit*, *The Searchers* and *The Alamo*. John was our hero; he epitomised rugged masculinity with his distinctive voice, walk and height. He had become an enduring American icon, and to us – pre-adolescent boys on the tip of Africa – he became the model of the men we wanted to be.

After each movie we'd walk home copying the John Wayne cowboy, bandy-legged stagger. The cinema brought back classics like *Stagecoach* and *The Wings of Eagles*. We also loved Gregory Peck, Steve McQueen and James Stewart, but Wayne was our boy.

Besides the cowboy movies, a favourite movie at the time was *The Great Escape*. It starred Steve McQueen and Charles Bronson and was a Second World War movie based on true events about the Allied Forces in a prisoner-of-war camp. The story told of how the prisoners planned to escape by tunnelling under the fence around the camp. After seeing the film, we decided to dig a tunnel in my backyard. As soon as we got home, we got a couple of shovels and set to work. But we didn't expect the ground to be so hard – it was going to take longer than we'd thought! We didn't realise that the tunnel the two-hour movie had shown had taken those prisoners nearly two years to dig. With stoic determination we persisted. I didn't ask my mom for permission; we had to keep this a secret.

After a few days we ended up with a big hole of about four feet wide and three feet deep. We found some old planks, painted them and covered the hole. Then we placed sods of grass on top – the perfect camouflage. We had a lot of fun hiding in there from time to time over the next few months. Sometimes I used to climb into the hole just to get away from hearing my mother shouting at my father. Like all good things, our escape tunnel was eventually discovered: my mother came across it one day when one of us had forgotten to close it properly. She was horrified that we had dug up her garden without consulting her. She ranted. But then, after a couple of days, things went back to normal.

I could still get some of my friends to play these games with me in the early years of high school, but they were moving on fast and I was being left behind. Their preoccupations were all in the locker rooms – comparing size and strength and conquests. I was the baby at home, still playing cowboys and crooks.

Then Michael and Luis started asking girls to join our group outings to the cinema, which was a problem for me, as I didn't want to ask a girl for fear of rejection. I also didn't want to be the spare boy – the gooseberry. But Michael insisted on including me. When they later started going on their own with a date, I was left on the shelf, so to speak.

11

Holidays

The holidays brought some respite from the trials of growing up – or not doing so, in my case. As I got older – I was about fifteen – I was allowed to do more things indepently; maybe it was a relief for my parents to get rid of us boys for a few days. I used to go down to the Vaal River with my cousins, who ranged in age from thirteen to sixteen. My Aunt Joan drove a battered old Datsun bakkie with a canopy at the back that was much larger and higher than the normal ones, so we could all fit in quite easily – sleeping bags and all. In my aunt's family, there were four boys and three girls, but on these holidays only the boys came along – Desmond, Keith, Shaun and Wayne. Keith and I were good friends. He was a year younger than me; Desmond was a year older. Sometimes Desmond's friend, Mike, joined us.

Aunt Joan would drop us off at the river with a week's rations, tents, sleeping bags and food. It was an exhilarating time; we were independent and could go to sleep at whatever time we liked. We had access to a local farmer's canoes, as long as we left them as we found them. One canoe was unsinkable. It had two air pockets – one in the front and one at the back, and three of us could fit in it.

On one occasion there had been a lot of rain and many trees in the area were under water. One morning Keith, Desmond and I decided to do a bit of exploring. Shaun and Wayne stayed behind. We paddled around for about an hour before making our way back to the shore. We were about fifty metres from the shoreline when, as we paddled under the trees, we felt a plopping on our shoulders. Hundreds of huge spiders, each about the size of a fist, were falling on us, obviously using us as vessels to get to the shore. Screaming, we jumped out of the boat faster than the spiders had landed in it. Thank God the water wasn't very deep, and we managed to swim back with the boat in tow. As we reached the shore, the spiders jumped off and ran off into the grass. Boy, did we crap ourselves!

In December, my family usually went to Durban on our annual visit – such a highlight for us. My father's sister Ida and her husband James lived in Durban North, close to Virginia airport. We travelled by train. We each carried our own luggage – suitcases and all – first putting it on the bus for the thirty-minute ride to Johannesburg station, and then carrying it into the station building.

Johannesburg railway station used to be a couple of floors below the ground. We'd walk into an enormous entrance hall with tall glass windows. It was like an aeroplane hangar, with separate entrances inside leading to the various platforms.

Dad and I would try to find a porter to help us with luggage, while my mother would go off to get the tickets. We kids were so excited about it all; we couldn't wait to board the train.

In the late 1960s and early 1970s, South African Railways (SAR) used mostly steam engines; later they went on to diesel. I loved the steam engines – big, black, enormous and all shiny, with their brass polished and steam pouring out from the sides and the top. There was a smell about those steam engines, a combination of burning coal and smog, a bit like the scent when it was just about to rain.

We would board the train, and there was always a fight to decide who was going to sleep where. The compartments had three beds on either side that pulled out from the walls. The middle one was the best, because from there you could see through the compartment's window. The top bunk was very high and the bottom one was right below the window sill, where one could feel quite claustrophobic. This feeling would soon pass, as I learnt.

We would wait and listen to the 'choo' of the steam engines before they started to move. There was always a slight shudder as the train slowly started to pull away. Often the SAR used two steam engines to pull the coaches. At times I'd stick my head out of the window and get a blast of thick smoke and soot in my face.

The highlight of the trip was going to dinner in the dining car, with its heavy wooden tables, each with its own waiter. We would be served a full seven-course meal, starting with soup and ending with dessert. I tasted my first sole on the train; it was my father's favourite dish and soon became mine, too. The train trip would last about twenty-four hours. I remember the beautiful countryside as we neared Natal – something you don't see from a car. My uncle James – my father's brother-in-law – would meet us at Durban station. He'd pick us up in his black 16/60 Wolseley.

There was something about James: I often got the feeling that he was not impressed by my father or our family. I thought that he rather fancied himself; my father must have been seen as the misfit of the family because of his moods. We had to be on our best behaviour at the Kings' place – that was James's surname, and I think he thought he *was* one. The Kings rented the top part of a double-storey – three bedrooms and a very large, enclosed balcony. I will always remember the sweet, musky smell of their house, which I have never come across anywhere else; I wonder what it was. We would often stay there for two weeks at a time.

Ida and James had met each other during the Second World War up in North Africa. She was a lieutenant in the nurses' corps and James was a sergeant. Once, when they were having a drink with my mother and father, we kids were playing cards in the lounge and overheard a bit of a disagreement: Ida was reminding James that she had been a lieutenant in the war.

Durban at that time of the year was very hot. Temperatures often rose into the thirties. I remember the old Lido Hotel on the beach, the source of the best milkshakes. Dad treated us to one every once in a while. My favourite flavour was chocolate.

I used to love paddling in the ocean on a lilo, but my favourite pastime was surfing. I never had a surfboard, so I would just bodysurf – like a seal enjoying the power of the waves. I'd surf until I was completely exhausted; then it was time to find my parents. I sometimes got lost trying to get back to them when I came out of the water, as I'd had to leave my glasses on my towel when going into the water.

I would try to wade my way towards the beach in a straight line to reach my towel, but the waves would push me around so that, when I finally came out, I would have been knocked off course. As I was so short-sighted, everything on the beach was just a blur. I'd find my parents eventually, but I was always anxious swimming alone. Later, certain landmarks helped me to establish my whereabouts, but I still got lost now and again.

I was not only self-conscious about wearing glasses, but also about my body. The other guys – my cousins and my sister's friends – all looked good in their swimming trunks. I was the skinny little guy who looked much younger than he was. A well-known advertisement during my childhood featured a weak, unconfident teenager having sand kicked in his eyes, and then being transformed into a strong, self-assured man after eating Black Cat peanut butter. It didn't matter how much peanut butter I ate, I remained a scrawny chap like the one who had sand kicked in his eyes. I was never going to turn into a superhero.

But the holidays flew by – it seemed that no sooner were we having a good time than we were heading back home until the following year.

A few years later we again went to Durban on the train, but this time we stayed in hotels. I am not certain if this was because there was friction at Ida and James's place, but we, as a family, never stayed there again. When I was older, I stayed with Ida and James for about a week, and I was reminded of those old memories and smells. They would remain with me for a long time.

12

The best of times
and the worst of times

My high school years were both the best of times and the worst of times: however much I loved hanging out in Rhodes Park or in the street with my friends, I hated both home and the classroom. At home, my parents fought continually. As usual, my dad's condition made him unpredictable and moody, and my mother, exhausted from holding down two jobs, often lost her composure. If she wasn't screaming at him, she was angry with one of us.

It was even worse at school. Every hour I spent there was a struggle. I still could not seem to absorb any of the lessons, and, as in primary school, the words 'stupid' and 'lazy' came up many a time. What was left of my self-esteem was peeled off layer by layer. I was slipping into an abyss. I had no idea how to change any of this or why it was happening. My classroom experience was like a long sigh. Every time a question came round to me, I tensed up. Would I know the answer? Sometimes I did and I'd put my hand up and wave, but the teacher wouldn't see me or would ignore me. I wondered if she passed me by so I couldn't get the answer wrong.

When she did respond to my raised hand, she'd say, 'What now, Stephen?' By this time I'd have the attention of the whole class. Then I'd find myself stuttering. This amused the class no end, and, now embarrassed beyond words, I'd say nothing at all. Eventually I did not participate in class at all. As mentioned, I went right through high school not taking part in any school sport either.

As for my studies, I was told that I had to work on my memory retention. I would read the pages over and over again. In my head I had all the answers and believed I could get a distinction for the subject, but the moment the exam papers were put in front of me and I tapped into the memory bank, nothing came out. I often ended up guessing the answers to get through. I tried to use 'donkey bridges' (mnemonics) to help me remember, but that didn't work either.

By now I was convinced that I was stupid. After all, I had been told I was stupid often enough by teachers over the years. Maybe it was true. But years later, as an adult, when I was study-ing anatomy and physiology, multiple-choice questions were used in the tests. This, I discovered, was a much better method for me. The lecturer believed that, had I been tested with mul-tiple-choice questions at school, my life choices might have been very different.

So, school work was very difficult for me. I know this might seem like the usual story of a kid not doing too well at school, but all the events that occurred had a long-term effect on my life. Yet I plodded on, managing to just scrape through each stan-dard. When I finally got to Standard 8, my parents felt it would be best if I left school and qualified in a trade. Bang went my biggest dream: I had always loved animals, and my strongest desire was to become a veterinary surgeon. When I was a toddler, we had a family dog named Sandy – a fox terrier. I was particularly fond of her, even though I would pull her ears or tail while whispering endearments into her ear. Fortunately, like most good-natured dogs, she took it in her stride.

All my friends were now showing obvious signs of puberty.

My life continued unchanged, but I noticed the differences between my friends and me. They were growing both upwards and sideways, and were starting to develop muscles – I noticed how my friends' arms and legs seemed to have so much more definition than mine.

They also had hair growing in all the right places. In the locker room, they would compare their progress. Some precocious blokes were even shaving. I'm sure some were bluffing and shaving in order to encourage hair growth, but they all examined each other's cheeks for the first signs of a beard. They'd look at my peachy cheeks and run a hand over them. 'Just bumfluff,' was the verdict.

All my friends' voices were breaking and they were all emitting strange rasping noises. I was still a soprano, but I wasn't auditioning for the Drakensberg Boys' Choir. My mom tried to reassure me, telling me that everyone was different. She must have worried too and noticed my concern about my high-pitched voice.

'You'll catch up by matric, you'll see,' she'd say.

The first time I noticed anything was seriously amiss with me was when I felt some discomfort in my groin. There was a pain just below the pelvic bone, as if somebody had kicked me, a bit like a stomach pain. Then I noticed a slight bump above my penis (little boys panic about this sort of thing, as do all men). The pain was worse when I sat down. When I ran my fingers around my testicles, I noticed that there was one missing. I could feel the sweat pouring over my face. I felt the rising panic; where could it have gone?

I started running my hand around the area, trying to follow the path to where it could be. And there it was – about four inches above the penis. I tried to gently push the testicle down to my scrotum. It required a bit of patience, but I didn't have to do this for long, as the next thing, it slipped back in. There was a lot of discomfort for about half an hour. Sometimes it took me longer to slip it back into place, and I knew that eventually something would have to be done. I approached my mother about this very shyly. She, in turn, asked my father to talk to me and have a look. He confirmed the situation, and my mother made arrangements to take me to the children's hospital.

It was the beginning of another round of doctors' visits with my mother. One doctor found that there was indeed a problem with my testicles. He said one testicle was an ascending testicle (an *offending* testicle!). It was not an unusual condition: 'Fairly common in young boys,' the doctor reassured us. He explained that the testicle sometimes fails to come down and remains in the groin area.

But six months later it had still failed to descend, so he decided to perform an operation to help it on its way. The op to the right testicle was, fortunately, a success.

What about the other testicle? Another doctor told my mother, 'I don't think he'll be able to have children due to the size of his testicles.' No one said anything else was amiss. The doctor didn't refer me to a specialist or elaborate on the condition. There is no blame to be laid here; I was just an anomaly.

Thank God I wasn't interested in girls at that stage, and they weren't interested in me either. Who knows, they might have been sympathetic. I knew it was a matter of time before the issue of girls would arise – girls were all my friends seemed to talk about. They were just lucky – these early developers.

Deep down, however, I knew all was not well with me. I knew I wasn't homosexual, as I had never had feelings for boys. I did have a fluttering of interest in girls, but my fear kept me from showing them. Something else entirely was the matter; I thought I must be a freak. My feelings of being different, and possibly even abnormal, threatened to overwhelm me. I didn't feel able to speak to my mother (I mean, boys don't talk to their mothers about those things) or my father. Would one of them notice I had a problem? I always undressed as privately as I could and tried to convince myself, 'Everything will be okay.'

Unbeknown to me, my mother, bless her, had continued to be concerned. She tried to talk to me, but I was too shy.

'Don't worry, Ma. Everything's fine,' I assured her. By then I was sixteen and hadn't grown beyond the five-foot-one mark, and, as I mentioned before, I weighed only ninety-four pounds. So my mother insisted on the doctor route again – a decision that would haunt me for years to come.

PART TWO

Of superheroes, small guys
and beardlessness

13

No smooth ride

What work would I be able to do after school? I was flailing. My marks were low; my learning problems had caught up with me and I realised that I would not pass the matriculation exams. Perhaps if I'd been at a school offering more insight, understanding and support, I could have got my matric, or Senior Certificate. I've already mentioned that I had wanted to train as a vet. I'd always loved animals – as an entry from my mother's journal, written when I was four, shows:

> I bought Stephen a little white mouse a few months ago and he absolutely adored it. Although he was rough sometimes with it too, he used to even sleep with it or when you took it away at nights, he would wake up and say, 'Where is my mouse?' During the day he would sometimes remember that the mouse had to eat in between playing with it, and he would say, 'Come little Mousie, you must come and have your foodies now.' He would have enough food in the mouse box for ten mice. Sandy (our dog) unfortunately caught it and put its eye out. Soon afterwards the mouse was found dead on the steps and nobody knew how it had died. I have an idea that it was Sandy but I was at work and didn't know how upset Stephen was, because twice before when it had got lost and was found again, he cried bitterly. I am going to buy him one again soon.

Training to be a vet would have required a university-entrance matric with science and maths. In the end, it was decided that I would have to abandon my dream and leave school with a Junior Certificate. I would follow a trade.

My mother was still concerned about the fact that I wasn't 'growing up'. She began the doctor trail again, dragging me from one to another. And the doctors' refrain?

'Don't worry – he'll start growing when he reaches eighteen. He is just a person of small stature with boyish looks. He'll grow out of it.'

But my mother persisted. She set up an appointment with a doctor new to the area. Even before she had finished explaining, the doctor seemed to recognise some of the symptoms and said, 'There seems to be a problem ... and possibly an abnormality for his age.' He recommended that we see another specialist.

So, the following week, off we went to see an endocrinologist – endocrinology is a branch of medicine that deals with disorders of the endocrine system and, specifically, hormones. Both my mom and I were incredibly relieved: we had found someone who actually understood and believed us. This was a happy day for me – perhaps the beginning of a new life. Little did I know that this appointment and the many that would follow held some nasty surprises.

As I entered the consulting rooms, I suddenly felt uneasy. I couldn't put my finger on it, but it was more a gut feeling of discomfort (not that I ever felt elated when doctors ogled me). I knew that I would have to take off my clothes; the feeling of having a strange person looking at my body was very embarrassing. (It was embarrassing enough when I was skinny-dipping in Rhodes Park lake with my *friends* and they ended up laughing at me. The mere thought of an *adult* looking at me was even worse. His being a doctor made no difference – he was still a man.)

Although I understood the need to remove my clothes for the examination, as always a sense of panic ran through me, only this time more intense. I was both mortified and shy – a sixteen-year-old with the body of a ten-year-old. And I was terrified. What was the specialist going to do? He connected electrodes to my body – sticky plastic patches attached to wires that led to a machine on which he could monitor the data.

All the while, as he was checking on the machine, his eyes seemed to run up and down my penis. Was he looking at me? I told myself that he was the doctor and that, most probably, he had to observe me this intensely. I was still terribly embarrassed. I understood that, as my sexual organs were the problem, he would have to examine them, but I found myself almost blacking out with fear. Unfortunately there was nowhere for me to run; I had to endure the examination. The specialist reached down to between my legs, took my testicles in his hand and felt them. I shut my eyes tightly as he squeezed my most private places. Then he told me to get dressed and called my mother. He told her that he would require more tests and asked if I could return for another appointment the following week.

We left. My mother tried to take my mind off things and offered to buy me a milkshake. I just wanted to get home. I hated this – why did I have to be different? What was wrong with me? And, above all, why did a man have to hold my testicles?

The following week we returned to the specialist's rooms. Once again I had to take my clothes off and lie down. I had the same queasy feelings I had had the week before, and felt an intense dislike of the doctor. After the first appointment I had thought it was normal to dislike a stranger squeezing one's testicles, but now I felt there was something very wrong.

The doctor leant over me and, without looking me in the eye, reached for my groin. I rolled my eyes backwards into my head in an effort to escape this awful man and this terrible place. But I had nowhere to go. His hand was between my legs and I felt him touching my testicles – I am sure his hand stayed there for far too long.

Then he took my penis in his hand and stroked it. 'Is this normal?' I thought. No matter how apprehensive I felt, I could not muster the courage to question him, let alone challenge him. I had grown up in a society where children never stood up to adults and certainly never said 'no' to them. How was I supposed to remain calm? He was invading my privacy. And my worst fear was about to occur – I felt my penis becoming erect.

I was red in the face, but as hard as I tried, thinking of all sorts of distractions, I could not reverse the sensation. I rolled my eyes back into the reality of the room and the doctor with the creeping hands and turned my head away. Out of the corner of my eye I sensed, rather than saw, a smile cross his face. After what seemed like days (the consultation lasted an hour), the session was over.

'That's all for today and I need to see you in a week's time,' he said.

I left, unsettled and confused. I knew that my mother would ask how it went. What did I tell her? I lied: 'Everything was fine, Mom.' I felt dirty. I went home and agonised. Was it something *I* had done? Had I done something wrong? Was I abnormal in other ways too? Why did he touch me like that; why did he look at me the way he did? I could not come to terms with him touching and ogling my body.

A week later, I returned. Would he do what he'd done before? 'Surely not,' I thought. I tried to believe that somehow the doctor needed to do what he did in order to diagnose what was wrong with me. It was part of the medical procedure, and so it had to be appropriate. I longed to ask my mother whether the docter's actions were normal and for her to come into the examination room with me and not to wait outside, but how could I? I was sixteen; she and the doctor would tell me I was being a baby.

I sat in the waiting room, squirming. Eventually the doctor came out of his rooms and nodded in my direction. He gave nothing away. Maybe it was all going to be fine this time. 'This time he will not do what he did before,' I thought. Inside the consulting room, and without a flicker of emotion on his face, the doctor told me to undress and lie down on the bed. I reluctantly took off my clothes. When I turned, I saw the doctor standing there, silently watching me. I left my underpants on and began to climb onto the bed.

'No, sonny,' he said. 'Everything.'

I felt extremely anxious, but mutely I obeyed. The docter started asking me embarrassing questions: Did I masturbate? Did I fantasise about girls? His face lit up. He squeezed my arms and legs, pushed on my muscles, prodding all the time, and then he put his hand on my penis. I just lay there feeling numb; a kind of blindness came over me, as if I was going to faint. I wanted the room to disappear, him to disappear, for it all to just go away.

The doctor ran his hand up and down my penis. I knew this wasn't right, but I was unable to move. He continued asking me questions. Although I tried to answer, my voice came out like a low bark, so I kept quiet. He kept his hand on my penis as his mouth formed a narrow smile. I wanted to die. My sexuality was a private matter, and something I never talked about to anyone. Now an adult had infiltrated this very private world, messing it up. These would be my memories of my first sexual experiences. I was angry, but fear and guilt paralysed me.

For the next few weeks I returned to see the doctor and each time we went through the same routine. I dreaded every moment. To my horror, he asked that the visits be increased to twice a week. I asked my mother why he wanted to see me so often, and, although she also found it odd, she went along with it: 'After all, he should know, he is the doctor.' I would have to continue seeing him until he had completed the tests.

All the examinations followed the same pattern. The little smirk crossed his face each time my penis became erect – I can still see his face to this day. He obviously gained extreme pleasure from the abuse.

After six months, the sessions finally came to an end. And he pronounced that I had a condition called Klinefelter's syndrome. Of course I had no idea what Klinefelter's syndrome was, and neither did my mother. But I felt a great sense of relief that I finally knew what was wrong with me. All those doctors' visits had finally ended in a diagnosis.

Although I no longer had to see the abusive specialist, the scars would remain for a very long time. Looking back now, even though I knew at the time that there was something very sinister about the way I was being examined, I didn't question it. After all, he was the doctor and my mother was in the waiting room. 'How could a specialist abuse his power?' I thought. My mind twisted the facts so that I believed I was abnormal in some way and so deserved the treatment. Deep down, though, I knew what he had done was wrong. I felt guilty and dirty. In a way, that made me feel worse, and I buried my feelings deeply. I thought I could forget it, but each time I would have a sexual encounter as an adult, I felt diminished. I agonised over my penis being big enough, if I could perform normally, or if I was just a freak.

The specialist referred me back to my general practitioner, who would from then on give me monthly testosterone injections, as my body was (and still is) unable to produce sufficient testosterone on its own. It was explained to me that the testosterone supplement would mimic the natural testosterone cycle and improve my self-confidence, increase my energy levels, enhance mood stability and concentration, and improve my social skills.

The course of injections would last for the next two years and, apart from the changes I mention above, would make my body more like those of other boys my age. I would grow taller, and I would also grow underarm, pubic and facial hair! In time, I would be like other boys my age.

However, the effects took a while to kick in (naturally, I wanted to see results overnight). And so my life carried on much as before – at least initially. I still longed to catch up with the other boys and feel normal.

Looking back now, I wish there had been more literature available on Klinefelter's syndrome at the time I was diagnosed. My mother, for example, likened it to Down's syndrome, because of the extra chromosome. And the doctors, including our own GP, knew little more than Mom. My family wasn't too bothered by the diagnosis, but today, I wish I had been diagnosed much earlier. It would have explained so much that had bothered me over the years, and if I had had the testosterone injections earlier, who knows how different my life would have turned out? I might have sailed through school; I might have chosen a different career. I think I could have coped with life a whole lot better. Who knows?

14

The seventies

Although it had begun working its subtle magic, the testosterone still hadn't taken complete effect. I hadn't really noticed any major changes. Deep in the tissues of my body there must have been shifts, but still I was small and underdeveloped. Besides, I was trying to forget what had happened in the endocrinologist's room. More than ever before my sexual development was a thing of embarrassment to me.

In the meantime, being a teenager in the Johannesburg of the 1970s was an exciting adventure and somewhat distracted me from what was happening to my body.

I was as politically naive as I was sexually naive; I was unaware that millions of my countrymen had a very different reality from mine. My obsession at that time was the big cinemas going up everywhere in Johannesburg. These were modern theatres – the Metro Theatre in Commissioner Street, the Kine Centre in Twist Street, the Highpoint in Hillbrow, and Ster City near Doornfontein – nothing like the old bioscopes.

These newly built theatres had the latest technology. They were the first to have big speaker systems installed, seated a couple of hundred people and featured bars where we could sit and have a few drinks before the show. They were *the* place to go to on a Friday or Saturday night.

One of the movies I remember well is *Sleeper*, starring a very young Diane Keaton and Woody Allen, which the Metro

Theatre in Commissioner Street chose for its grand opening – an affair to attend. They rolled out the red carpet and invited all the local celebrities.

We also went to see the great war movies, like *The Guns of Navarone*. Because the sound systems were so advanced, with surround sound, the building actually shook with gun blasts and bomb explosions. I'll never forget seeing *Earthquake*. The sound was so loud and all-encompassing, it made us shake in our seats and created a virtual experience of a quake.

Movies opened at the new Kine theatres first and afterwards made their way to the smaller movie houses in the suburbs. On Saturday afternoons, Luis and I would catch a bus into town to my favourite theatre, the spectacular Colosseum, a wonderful building constructed in Johannesburg's early years. Situated on the main street of Johannesburg, it was built in classical style, with columns on either side. It looked a bit like its Roman namesake and was used for both live stage shows and movies. The interior was done up like a castle courtyard, with little globes set into the ceiling to represent stars. Upstairs there were Juliet balconies, and an usher would take your tickets at the door. He had a thick, sharp spike onto which he pushed the ticket and then threaded it down onto a string.

An usherette would show us to our seats. The stage of the Colosseum had enormous red curtains that covered the screen, and thick red carpets – real old-style. I saw some great acts there as a kid, among them Cilla Black – she was very popular in the early 1970s – and The Troggs, when they toured from England. They were a fairly noisy band, and one of their songs, 'Wild Thing', was my favourite. I loved it back then and everybody went mad when they performed it. But over the years I've come to hate this song. It was overkill; every radio station would play it. There were times when I went out with some friends to a local bar or club, and it seemed that every time I walked in, that song was playing.

Then, all of a sudden, while all this was going on, the testosterone kicked in, taking me completely by surprise. Out of the blue, my planet was invaded by alien creatures: I began to notice women in a whole new way. The shutters on my eyes were lifted. One Saturday I met a girl at Michael's house. I really liked her, and she seemed to like me too. I tentatively asked her out, and she said yes. I had a girlfriend!

Theresa was my first love. She had mousy blonde hair and was slightly plump, but that didn't bother me. She was only about five foot four, but wherever she went, she turned people's heads. (I wasn't much taller than her then, as I hadn't quite begun my growth spurt.) Theresa just had something about her – a kind of glow. She was my first real encounter with a girl. At high school I'd shied away from girls because I was so embarrassed by my size. But with the testosterone injections, I was feeling a whole new world opening up to me. I became sexually more revved up than I had ever been.

On one of our first dates, Theresa and I went to a concert at the Colosseum. It was a one-off act – a local band from Pretoria. I had been rather embarrassed to tell my friends that I was going to this concert – the band was new and I thought my friends would dismiss it and my taste for music. Well, I was wrong. The show was fantastic. The band was known as Rabbitt, and it went on to become extremely popular. One member, Trevor Rabin, was a great songwriter, and is now known also for his movie soundtracks.

Theresa and I dated for about fifteen months. We'd kiss and pet each other lightly, but nothing more than that. Our restraint was a combination of my insecurities and a fear of her traffic-cop father.

I had got my first motorbike. When I met Theresa's family, they didn't mind the bike, as other girls' parents may have done, as Theresa's father also rode bikes. On weekends, Theresa's brother would get out his scrambler to go and ride in the countryside. But if riding a bike was not a problem for Theresa, something else was: after a year or so I discovered that Theresa was two-timing me. Of course I blamed myself, thinking that she probably wanted more of a sexual relationship. I, however, was still too timid. I was convinced my penis wasn't big enough, or that she'd find fault with me somehow. And so we split up.

I was too embarrassed to tell Luis and Michael that Theresa had two-timed me, so I pretended that I simply didn't like her any more. I continued to hang around with my male friends, but things were no longer the same. While I made do with their company, I actually longed for love and a girlfriend who would make me feel confident. I was plagued by my insecurities, a situation that would last for a long while. I had no idea that my penis was now a completely normal size. Who would have told me? And I had other problems lurking. So I fell back on the friendships that had carried me thus far.

Luis and I loved playing pinball at the shops. The point of the game was to accumulate as many points as possible while keeping the metal ball in play. I remember my first game, walking up to that huge machine with its flashing lights. Other boys were also playing, which I was a bit nervous about. These boys were older than me, and I watched as they gyrated their hips while manipulating the flippers. I placed my money on the side of the pinball machine and waited my turn. By the time it came, I was sweating. I pulled back on the plunger and released it. I watched in amazement as the metal ball shot up into the playfield and the score started running up. But the ball only bounced around for a few minutes and, before I could use the flippers, went straight down the middle. The game had lasted for only about two minutes, but it had been a huge accomplishment for me to play for the first time with all the older kids watching.

We soon graduated to snooker. In those days we could still go to snooker clubs in town and have a great time. The clubs were fairly close to Jeppestown, which, although somewhat industrial, had some office buildings too. Still, it wasn't the best part of town. The club we used to go to was situated below a shop. As we walked in, we'd get stares from the locals. Initially that made us a bit nervous, but eventually we'd be accepted.

The place had about twenty full-size snooker tables, over which cigarette smoke hung like curtains. Just about everybody smoked then. It was a bit like walking into a jazz club in New Orleans, but without the live music. There were overhead speakers and the place was fairly dark; the tables were lit by low ceiling lights. Some clubs also had their own bars. I never saw a fight take place. There was an understanding, sort of like a secret code: nobody came over to challenge you. It took real skill to play snooker.

Tea-room bioscopes also featured in Johannesburg at the time. One had to walk through the tea room to go into the smoke-filled theatre, which was about twenty square metres in size – in those days one could smoke in the bioscopes too. The seats inside were dark red, and each had a long shelf in front of it, attached to the back of the chairs in the row ahead – like a mini bar counter – that held one's beer, lunch or ashtray.

Once you had paid to enter, you could sit there watching movies the whole day. They changed movies about three times a day. You'd often find some creepy types there too. A new friend, Antony, and I used to go together. He said he would 'educate' me. I would never have found one of those places on my own; they were quite difficult to locate. But Antony sure found them! I went to these tea-room bioscopes only once or twice. They weren't exactly places I would take my first date to, but all the same I'm glad I saw them with my own eyes.

The other bioscopes in our area were the Gem and the Regent. The Gem was in Troyeville, which was more like 'Divesville' – a place where only the scum of the earth would risk going. There was always a fight there; in fact, a fight was one of the highlights of going there and why thugs liked the place. You pretty much entered at your own risk. The Gem had two levels; the upper level had a wing or balcony, which stuck out about halfway over the lower level. Only the thugs sat upstairs.

I once went to the Gem because it showed great Westerns. I decided to take the risk so I could see *The Magnificent Seven*, starring Yul Brunner. 'It can't be as bad as some of the stories I've heard,' I thought. When I got there, I tried to go upstairs, but the woman at the ticket booth said it was full. I took a seat downstairs, just beneath the overhang. Thank goodness I chose that seat, because, within minutes of the lights going out, popcorn and Coke bottles started flying over the balcony. Then somebody got hurt. There was both screaming and laughter.

The ushers ran upstairs and tried to find the culprit, but this only resulted in a physical fight. Only halfway through the movie did things calm down.

I much preferred the more upmarket Regent. It was in Kensington, only about ten kilometres from the Gem, but middle- to upper-class people frequented the Regent. The chance of any scum going to movies there was unlikely – it wasn't exciting enough for them.

The Regent was on one level, so no bottle-throwing here. The one movie that sticks in my mind and made an impact on me was *Woodstock*. Seeing this film was the highlight of my young life; it was the essence of the youth culture. It encapsulated the energy, rebellion and anger of the time. The artists, the music and the movie summed up the cult of the 1970s. I loved both the music and how the American youth rebelled against their government. Both these elements gave a voice to the rage I felt against so much of the patriarchal society I lived in – the teachers, my school and the looming army.

The army. The time had come to face the music. As a young man in South Africa, I was left with no choice. The year was drawing to an end – and it was the end of school for me. I had elected, under pressure disguised as advice from my parents and teachers, to leave at the end of Standard 8. I would sit the exams and, if I passed, I would receive a Junior Certificate. I was hoping to go on and study something practical, something that would make me feel useful and able. But what? I was sixteen, but small and puny, more like a thirteen-year-old. I wasn't ready for the world of work. But I didn't have to think of that yet. Something else was waiting for me – and though I certainly wasn't ready for it either, I was 'man' enough for it: the army.

15

Military training

When I was halfway through Standard 8, I got my call-up papers. We all knew we'd be called up, and were all waiting for our papers to arrive. If you were still a student, they would come through the school, which informed the military who would be finishing school that year – but on rare occasions the papers came in the post. We all dreaded receiving those bloody papers. I was hoping to be overlooked. Although the testosterone had begun affecting my hormones, there were no physical changes. I was still small. I'd not yet started growing, let alone shaving.

But it was the law of the land – if you left school, you were eligible for call-up. I didn't want to go to the army or fight for my country. Clouds of war were gathering on the border – the government was preparing to defend the country against the 'terrible' communists, *die rooi gevaar* (the red danger). The propaganda machines were working overtime to brainwash us into war. I knew it was all bullshit, although I didn't understand the complexities then. But I did know that this wasn't my darn war.

My brother had entered the air force a few years before, and he'd had a fantastic time during his nine-month stint. But he also terrorised me with stories of the horrors and hardships. All in all, he made it sound as glamorous as the war movies I loved: it was a way to become a man. But I was terrified.

I had to choose what part of the Defence Force I wanted to

serve in, so I decided on the air force. Some choice! In 1974 you could still choose your unit, but the authorities sent you anywhere they liked anyway. The first military item I got was my army number. As I was walking out of my last class, my teacher, Mr Henning, called me over. He had a funny look on his face. I thought he might be going to give me a mouthful about the subject at hand, but that look on his face told me that this was about something entirely different. He handed me a brown envelope and said, 'I think this is for you. I know it's not what you wanted, but good luck!'

'Good luck? What are you talking about?' I thought. It was three months before I would finish school, but I knew what was coming. I flipped the envelope over and looked at the back; the big bold letters 'DEFENCE FORCE – WEERMAG' jumped out at me. This was it. In the next couple of weeks I would receive the other papers telling me where I would be going – air force, navy or army.

It's a strange feeling when you are forced to accept your fate. You have no control over what will happen to you next. This is the feeling I had, waiting for those papers that would seal my destiny. Weeks passed. Eventually, one day, when I came home from school, a brown envelope lay on the half-moon table – the kind with the old ball-and-claw legs – that stood in our hallway.

I looked at the envelope, and again those bold letters jumped out at me: 'DEFENCE FORCE – WEERMAG'. I held my breath for a split second and then opened the envelope. There were three columns, each marked with the different categories. I scanned the page. My heart jumped: there was a tick in the air force column. I had been accepted into the air force! What a relief: of all the units, this was by far the best one. My friends and I had heard horror stories about the army, so going to the air force was a bonus. I felt a little bit of relief.

The next few weeks went by fairly quickly. The Defence Force had two intakes – in January and July. I was to go in January.

The night before I was due to leave, my mind was in turmoil, and I had a constant, nagging pain in my stomach. I didn't get much sleep either. Eventually night turned to day, and soon I would be heading off. Johnny and a friend of his, Neville, said that they would drive me to the camp. I said goodbye to my mother and Christine. My father wasn't home at the time; he had been suffering from a long bout of depression and was in hospital. The doctors were treating him at Tara, a psychiatric hospital north of Johannesburg, where he would stay for a few months. I suppose I'd got used to him being away from home, but I would have loved to have seen him that morning.

My mother and Christine were crying as they hugged me goodbye, and I so desperately wanted to hug them and hold on to them forever, but I told them everything would be fine. I put on a brave face, trying not to cry in front of Johnny and Neville.

As I walked towards the front gate, I heard 'A Whiter Shade of Pale' playing on the radio, and I went pale with fear. But I climbed into Neville's maroon Alfa Romeo, smiling bravely. The three of us waved goodbye to the women and drove off. I felt that I was never going to see my mother, sister and father again.

As the road led me away from my home and closer to Pretoria, I looked out of the window and tried to take in as much of the neighbourhood as possible, so that I would not forget where I came from. We drove down Clacton Road, past Luis's house. School had begun, so he wasn't there. Then past the house of Judy, the girl who had teased me.

Michael, although older than me, was also still at school. How I envied him this as I looked at his house at the end of the road. The car turned out of the neighbourhood and headed towards Bez Valley and the airport road. I stared out the window and saw the top of the hill and the castle we'd played in as kids. Then it all became too much; I sat there not saying a word. The other two chatted away happily, exchanging stories of their days in the air force. I just listened numbly to their conversation.

The drive seemed to take ages. Eventually we reached the gates of Valhalla, just outside the bigger base of Voortrekkerhoogte. Valhalla was better known as Valhalla Beach, but it was nothing like a beach on this occasion. The morning was hot and dry. A screen of dust raised by a thousand feet rose in the air and I stared through it as though watching a terrible movie. Then, through the dust emerged hundreds of scared faces just like mine. I had to get out of the car. Johnny was almost shouting at me, 'What's your problem? We're here. Get your bags.'

I grabbed my things, muttered a goodbye to Johnny and then looked around me. After the two officers at the gate had sworn and laughed at me, they asked to see my papers, which I showed them, with my number: 73277238. It's amazing how, well into my fifties, I still remember it. The officers told me to get in line. There were hundreds of guys like me, confused and disorientated. Orders were shouted from all over the place. Eventually somebody used a loudspeaker to tell the new guys to go to the parade ground. They yelled for us to *move*.

The next moment we were all running over to the parade ground, a massive open space, covered in reddish sand. By now, it was unbearably hot. Everybody was dripping with sweat. It ran into my eyes. I had to take off my glasses each time to wipe my face.

Some people obviously didn't believe in using deodorant, so the stench of the sweet, stale sweat was everywhere. The place smelt like a miner's armpit. We were told to form lines by putting our arms out in front of us, then move them to the side so that you just touched the person in front of you. That was how you got the correct distance between you. My arm reached only to the person's backside and hip bone, unlike the others, who could touch the shoulder of the man next to him. We stood there for about two hours waiting for the commandant to arrive. Some guys fainted in the heat of the sun – they just fell down as if somebody had hit them. There wasn't a cloud in the sky; the temperature was into the thirties on that awful day. Eventually the commandant arrived. He spoke a load of shit for the next hour and then put the young corporals back in charge of us.

The first couple of hours were total chaos, with everybody running around like a headless chicken. Orders rang out, but nobody seemed to know what to do or where to go. The shouting added to the confusion. We were eventually sent to the stores to fetch our *trommels* and *varkpans*. A *trommel* was a metal trunk, approximately 60 × 30 × 30 centimetres, issued to everyone in a new intake. It had two handles on either side and was for our odds and ends, like shoe polish, shoe brushes and cloths.

I immediately had a problem – I couldn't pick mine up; my arms were too short to reach down both the sides to lift it. I stood there, completely helpless. A vicious little corporal came over and asked me what the hell I thought I was doing. I tried to explain, but he just frothed at the mouth and shouted to two others to help me. They placed my *trommel* on top of theirs and carried it to the barracks. By that point I was proving to be popular: they eyed me out and told me they would get me. 'Great move,' I thought – I had been there only a couple of hours and already I had made enemies.

The corporals were sadistic bastards. The power the little pricks had over everybody was quite amazing, a bit like a prison system. The hours dragged on. At around midday, we went to eat our first lunch – 'slops' would be a more apt term. We discovered the use of the *varkpan*, which consisted of two oblong aluminium pans of approximately 15 × 20 centimetres, that served as both cooking pan and bowl. The handles could be folded back, allowing the two pans (one slightly smaller than the other) to fit into each other, making a closed container.

After lunch came the medical exam – everybody had to have a medical. Its aim was to sort us into different grades of fitness – G1 being the fittest and G4 the least fit. The examination began with a urine test. Some of the blokes mixed sugar with their urine; others mixed their pee with that of other men. I watched in utter amazement. All this was an attempt to get exempted. But the military was long wise to these ploys – nobody got away with this trick. There I was, thinking that I was the only one who wanted to get out of this shithole! I didn't have the courage to try these tactics, though.

We entered a big hall with various cubicles, with men queuing up in front of them. The staff told us to stand in a line to have our bodies examined. I was looking for a bit of privacy, but no – everybody had to witness the doctors grabbing our balls and asking us to cough! I think I was so embarrassed that a little murmur came out of my mouth. Not only did I feel small in stature, but also down there – there is no place like the Defence Force to make you face your issues. Next we moved on to the eye inspection. I waited for what seemed forever. Some chancers said they couldn't see the charts, but they were caught out. Finally my turn came.

'Walk up to the line and take off your glasses,' came the command. 'I want you to read the board.'

'What board? I can't see the board,' I said.

The doctor threatened that if I was pulling his leg, I'd better beware because I would end up in detention barracks. The mean-looking corporal nearby muttered. He came over to me and breathed hard into my face, his nose a snout.

'*Oppas, mannetjie. Jy moenie kak soek nie.*' ('Watch it, little boy. Don't look for shit.')

The doctor shooed him away and asked me to walk until I could see the board. I approached the board. I was about one foot away when I told him that I could now see the board and read the letters. The doctor shouted at me to come over to him so that he could examine my eyes. I sat in front of a funny contraption that magnifies your eyes and the doctor looked into them. He then asked me to look at some pictures so that he could test me for colour blindness. I passed that one, no problem, but he seemed rather concerned about my eyesight. He told me to wait a while until he could get somebody else to come and have a look at me. I didn't have to wait long before a tall, slim fellow arrived and asked me to sit down.

'Look to the left, look right, look up, look down,' he instructed me. Then he commanded, 'Stare straight ahead.'

Then yet another doctor came over to examine me. The result was the same each time. Each one shook his head. By now my eyes felt like somebody had shone a searchlight into them.

'Look up, look down, look right, left, don't blink.'

It was late afternoon by the time I left the medical rooms; I had been in there for a good four hours. I made my way back to the bungalow to which I'd been assigned and hoped I'd have time to rest. I was in for a few more hours of abuse, however. In the bungalow, the rest of my squadron asked me where I had been the whole afternoon. I filled them in.

Then a loud siren sounded. Time to go to the mess hall for dinner. The meals the air force served lived up to all I'd heard: the vegetables were overcooked; the meat looked like a stew of pig's slop. We learnt to eat it.

That night, as my head hit the pillow, I was gone. Gone, until the shouting of the corporals at five o'clock the next morning woke us up: 'Move! Move! Get your arses out of bed, get outside! Get to the parade ground.'

We were all red-eyed when we got there. The corporals did the roll-call and proceeded to teach us how to march. The sun wasn't even up yet. We bumped into each other in the dark. A lot of shouting and swearing followed. The best way to make a point was to add in a few 'fucks' here and there; that got people moving. We marched for the next two hours before we were instructed to go to the mess hall. The breakfast was as disgusting as dinner had been – the eggs were green. Afterwards, the corporals ordered us back to our bungalows to change into our PT shorts for some serious exercise.

I walked outside and joined my fellow recruits. We were assigned to different barracks and different squadrons. I was put into 2nd squadron, whatever that meant. The shouting from the little corporals didn't stop: '*Hardloop, julle fokken drolle!*' ('Run, you fucking shits!')

One particularly angry, red-faced corporal cast his eye on me. '*Wat!*' he yelled. '*Wat doen jy hier?*' ('What are you doing here?')

I was flustered, but tried to answer him. It just infuriated him more.

'*Sien jy daardie boom? Is jy al terug?*'

I didn't understand him and tried to ask him what he meant. Silly me. He blew his top. I just ran anyway.

My biggest fear had been that I couldn't speak Afrikaans. Unfortunately all the commands were in that language and I didn't have a clue what they meant, so in the few hours I had been there I found myself first in the wrong place and then in the wrong group. Eventually I befriended somebody who could speak both English and Afrikaans.

We went back to our barracks, where we were shown how to make up our beds – to the proper military standard. I couldn't understand why anybody would have to teach us to do this. Surely it is second nature? But no! In the air force we had to use our *varkpans* to make a bed. We had to sharpen the edges of our beds using two of these to make the edges square. Who gives a shit? Can you imagine bombs flying overhead and bullets whizzing past, but having to have your bed made up properly?

Lady Luck smiled on me then – my bed was chosen as the perfect example of a well-made-up bed. Everyone then had a go until all our beds were so perfect that nobody wanted to sleep on them. That night I slept under my bed, worried that I would never be able to get it as perfect again; I had heard so many terrible stories of punishment for chores not done correctly.

Sleep claimed me eventually, but not until I had lain awake for hours, wondering how I was going to survive the next two years. If nothing else, perhaps suicide was the only option. I couldn't imagine becoming one of these people who had no respect for their fellow human beings, no matter what their race or class. I started to realise that the people giving the orders were very different from anyone I had ever known.

Morning again seemed to come faster than I had ever thought possible. My short sleep was interrupted by bellowing voices shouting in Afrikaans, but this time I knew what it meant: 'Get out of bed! Move your arses! Stand to attention!'

With sleep still in my eyes, the corporals shouted at us to get down to the showers and clean up. Along with my squadron, I ran down the hill for about half a kilometre to the showers. To my horror, there was only one shower, which fifty men had to use. I have always had nightmares about this type of thing, being so shy about my body. Some men stripped down fast – it was a show-off contest for a few – but most of us were caught off guard. I made my way over to the furthest corner and took off my clothes, praying that nobody would notice me. Thank God that was the case. I think everybody was too concerned about themselves. We were in there for about five minutes when the order came to get out. That was fine with me.

We dressed and marched double quick to the mess hall for breakfast. Then more exercises, more abuse. The corporals were in their element. Left alone in charge of us, they hurled their orders about as we ran and marched and did endless push-ups. They seemed to thrive on screaming; every weakness they spied had them baying for blood. English-speaking soldiers were first in line for their terrible tongues.

'Jou blerrie rooinek! Jou fokken khaki. Ons sal jou wys wie het gewen.' ('You bloody redneck! You fucking khaki! We'll show you who won!')

I couldn't understand why they were raving, nor could I fathom the reference to the Anglo-Boer War. My father had links as far back as the early white settlers – just as their fathers had. Their war – or the shame of losing a war many decades earlier – seemed to drive them maniacally to prove they were men. My fellow English-speaking cadets and I were abused all morning, told to buck up or go back to England. This continued until we broke for lunch.

As I was making my way up to the bungalow with my squadron, a bloke came running up and began shouting out a name. At first I wondered who had done something wrong, but he was just calling someone, indicating that the person had to go down to the medical building. Then I registered that it was *my* name he was yelling.

'Malherbe! Malherbe! Where are you?'

I waved to the guy and called him over. He said the doctors wanted to talk to me. I found this odd, but who was I to argue? The commanding officer excused me. I made my way to the medical building. Questions raced through my mind: What could they possibly want with me? Had they picked up something else wrong with me? I was in a bit of a panic for the five minutes it took me to reach the building. I raced up the stairs, burst through the doors and made my way towards the doctors' rooms.

There, I was told I had to undergo more tests. It was my eyes again: a doctor asked me to remove my glasses and read the board. Again I couldn't see a thing. I squinted and even stretched my eyes wider, but all I could see were black smudges on white. I leant forward, further and further, until the doctor said, 'Step forward and stop when you can see the writing.' I shuffled forward. A foot nearer, another foot, but still the black smudges. I felt the doctor's eyes on me. I didn't want to be ridiculed for being so blind.

'Move until you can see the writing.'

Again I got to within a foot of the board.

'Doctor, I can now see the shape of the letters, but they are not clear.'

I waited for two hours for the non-military optician: more tests. Again I waited for the verdict. Finally, I was called in. Then, a miracle! The person told me I had been exempted.

'What? *Exempted*?' I asked.

He said not to ask any questions but to report to the commander's office, and gave me a piece of paper the commander needed to sign to release me. I was dumbfounded. I made my way slowly to the offices. Ten other men, who had also been exempted, were waiting there in a queue. We had all been classed G4 K4 (no-hopers).

After completing the paperwork, I returned to the bungalow to collect my things. The others were in the mess having their lunch, so I was alone. I looked around at the neatly made beds. I had not even slept in mine. I silently wished the others good luck and returned to the office.

The air force paid me one rand per day for the time I had spent there. I went over to the big, brown Bedford truck ready to take me and the other rejects on the half-hour journey to Pretoria station. Only when I got out of the truck and walked towards the ticket booth did it hit me that I had been saved.

I bought a one-way ticket to Johannesburg. Everything was a blur; the trip home went by extremely fast. Soon I was at Johannesburg station, where I caught the bus home. The scenes of my neighbourhood now swept by in reverse: the road from Bez Valley, the turning into Kensington, Michael's house and Luis's house. I took in the scenes around me, got off the bus and walked, in a daze, down the road back home.

I had thought I was going to die. But on 9 January 1975, the gods smiled on me. If I had died, who would have been responsible for my death – the authorities or me? Sadly, a lot of people I knew would either be killed or maimed in the armed forces.

Despite my relief at being released from the air force, I did have one concern: South Africans' rampant patriotism. Would I be seen in the eyes of many as a coward who hadn't served his country?

16

Apprenticeship

Back home again. Now I was done with both the air force and school. Neither had made me into the man society expected. I was seventeen now and not ready to take on the world, caught between childhood and adulthood, not able to make a living on my own. Whatever was I going to do? I wasn't sure what career to follow, since any hopes of studying to be a vet were gone. I was at my wits' end.

No one was around to support me. Luis and Michael were still at school; other friends were off to the army, university or apprenticeships in various fields. My parents were working. Johnny and Christine had both left home. Johnny had what seemed to me a glamorous job with South African Airways as an air steward and was flying all over the world. Christine worked at Standard Bank, where she was doing well and earning a fair salary. Sitting at home, I was reduced to the status of a preschool toddler. I had nothing to do, nor an inkling of what I should be doing.

My parents suggested an aptitude test, saying it would give me some guidance. But the idea of another test? It just gave me the heebie-jeebies. My mother set up an appointment a week after our conversation. She saw I was bored and frustrated not knowing what to do with my life, but that I was also afraid of yet another test.

I had expected the air force to keep me for two years, by which time I would have had more of an idea of what to do with the rest of my life. But, instead, I had to undergo another test. I kept asking my mother what type of test it would be, and she said not to panic; the test would merely indicate where my talents lay. She came with me when I went for the test – we caught yet another bus together, retracing the many trips we had taken since the early days.

The test took place at the Human Resource Institute in Johannesburg City. My stomach was in a knot; despite my mother's reassurances, I was panicking. Once we got to the offices, a woman took me into a room.

'Are you okay?' she asked.

'Yes,' I replied (though inside I was shouting, 'No! What am I doing here?').

She placed a form in front of me and told me to tick the answers to the questions on it. This wasn't so bad. I looked over the form quickly and proceeded to fill it in. It took about an hour. The woman returned, took the form and asked me to wait outside with my mother.

Mom asked how it had gone.

'It wasn't too bad,' I had to admit.

After a while we were called in to discuss the results. The woman said the tests suggested I should try becoming a panel beater or a plumber. Neither of the trades appealed to me, and I was horrified. Tests have never really helped me. Once again, because of the Klinefelter's syndrome, I couldn't express myself and I was misunderstood. I didn't want to be a panel beater. Surely there was something more appealing out there that I could do?

Shortly after taking the test, Luis told me that a company was looking for electricians. I applied and found myself on course to becoming an electrician. Unfortunately I only lasted about six months; the manager thought the job would be too strenuous for me. Then Johnny's friend William suggested I consider going into the printing industry – and that was the beginning of my working life.

I began by going from company to company in search of a job. I had a few interviews and eventually a company at the bottom of End and Durban streets took me on. I started my apprenticeship as a letterpress machine-minder, the last in line on the conveyor belt.

Before the start of a print job, we had to make sure that the ink ducts were set correctly and that the paper went through the machine properly – be it a newspaper, a book or some other publication. Other jobs in the industry included typesetting (compositing) and stripping films. I also had to learn to operate the different machines.

I learnt the trade on the job. The company also got me to enrol at the Johannesburg Technical College, where I did my N1 in printing – a practical course consisting of lithography, letterpress, mathematics and science.

It was a fresh start. I had a five-year apprenticeship contract in the printing industry, and all seemed to be going well. Some of my hang-ups also seemed to drop away, although I was now nineteen years old but still living with my parents. I invested in a new motorbike to get me to and from work.

But then, one fine morning, while I was on my way to work, a car jumped a stop street and collided with my motorcycle. I hit the driver's running-board, flew over my bike's handlebars and the bonnet of the car, and landed on the passenger side, virtually under the car's front wheel.

I stood up, feeling a bit bruised, but I didn't think anything was broken or that I even needed medical attention. Then, two hours later, the pain hit me; I have no recollection of anybody taking me to hospital, but that's where I woke up. X-rays revealed a broken bone in my foot and a chipped spine.

I was booked off work for six weeks, to the disgust of my company, as I had virtually just started my apprenticeship. I limped around and was in pain for many months. I initially presumed that the ongoing pain was the result of having had the foot and ankle in plaster for six weeks. But six months down the line, after more X-rays, doctors discovered that I had also suffered a broken hip.

The insurance company would not pay out, as the driver of the car had said *I* had jumped the stop street. The driver also managed to produce a false witness (the accident had occurred at 5.30 a.m., and there hadn't been a soul in sight). I was liable for the costs of the damage to his car as well as having to repair my motorbike. In order to pay for this little episode, I had to take out a loan – a big challenge on the wages of an 'appy' (apprentice). I was on a medical aid, so at least all the hospital costs were covered.

Another year passed. Life seemed to be picking up. But how wrong could I be! One day, happily working at the printing press, I experienced an excruciating pain in my right side. With great difficulty, I managed to drive to the hospital. I was told that my appendix was on the verge of bursting and had to be removed immediately.

Within minutes of my arrival, staff had given me an enema and I found myself on the operating table, about to receive a general anaesthetic and undergo an appendectomy.

'Everything is going to be all right,' the doctors reassured me.

Again I believed them, as I continue to do to this day.

My mother, who had been a nurse for a year, was still intrigued by anything medical. After the operation she took one look at the appendix in a bottle and then at the doctor.

She questioned him on the *pinkness* of the removed appendix: 'Doesn't it look perfectly normal to you? Strange that it would cause such pain.'

The doctor managed to persuade her that the appendix had been infected (too late anyway – it could not be reinserted!).

Two weeks later, the pain returned with almost the same intensity. Back I went into hospital, for more tests (and expenses), for the doctors to discover a duodenal ulcer. It's a pity they were so quick to operate the first time, or I would probably still have my appendix.

I continued to live at home – the apprentice wage was a pittance. I made new friends, though, and sometimes life was fun. In our area there were many new Portuguese immigrants from newly independent Angola and Mozambique. Historically, the south of Johannesburg had a large Portuguese population – wonderful, friendly people who stuck together.

I still hung out with Michael and Luis as well. It was the hippy era and young people lived together in communal houses. We went to many commune parties and met up with other friends at pubs. Often, we just sat around at home chatting.

I was still being given injections of testosterone on a monthly basis. The effects of the testosterone were gradual at first, but then, suddenly, the change was dramatic. My underarm hair started to grow. I had no facial hair as yet, but the best thing did happen: my voice dropped an octave and I didn't sound like a ten-year-old any more! I shot up like Jack's beanstalk: my height increased from five foot one to a staggering six foot in the space of eighteen months. I felt like I had grown wings! It was a wonderful feeling and I even gained a smidgen of self-confidence. Being taller made me feel great – I sympathise with short guys now.

I found the rush of new feelings both foreign and frightening. I began to grow more aggressive and was willing to punch anyone who upset me. My penis also grew, and it developed a life of its own, as the sexual urges I'd failed to feel for so long surged through my body.

I was like a snake shedding its skin. My clothes were suddenly too small; my shirts burst their buttons and the arm seams split if I bent down to pick something up. All my trousers were suddenly way too short for me. It took a while to adjust to the new me – a whole new person. I could now wear *men's* clothes, and I had to buy a whole new wardrobe.

For the first time in my life, I felt confident and powerful – the Black Cat boy had arrived at last – but my peanut butter was the testosterone! It surged through my body like a magic potion. At last I felt what all my friends had experienced in those locker rooms years ago.

A new girl, Cheryl, had moved into the neighbourhood, and Michael, Luis and I acted like the Three Musketeers, taking every possible opportunity to walk past her house, hoping to speak to her. But her house was hidden behind a high wall and the driveway was secured behind large wrought-iron gates. Also, her brother-in-law didn't like us, believing we were up to no good. Every time we had a moment, we tried to get her to chat to us outside her house or across the wall, but then he'd chase us away.

The brother-in-law was about ten years older than us – he

was big and strong and very protective of his sister-in-law (and his wife, of course). We hoped that one day she would see the light and come out on her own for a chat.

One night, Michael, Luis and I went to a party in the northern suburbs, scene of some of the best parties in Johannesburg. I picked them up in my first car, a Ford Escort – I had sold my bike and purchased the Escort in part-ownership with my mom. Afterwards, I dropped Michael at home and pulled up outside my house. Luis lived diagonally opposite me, and we were chatting about the babe down the road when we had a brainwave: we should weld the brother-in-law's gates permanently closed with a blowtorch! We knew Luis's dad had a blowtorch, but we weren't sure we'd get into the garage at that time of the morning without making a noise. We came up with another, much easier, plan: we'd remove his gates and leave them further down the road. This sounded like a fantastic plan, so off we went, laughing to ourselves.

We managed to lift one of the big black gates off quite quickly, but were rather taken aback by how heavy it was – especially after the few drinks we'd had. The other gate gave us more trouble, but eventually we managed to remove that one too. We were having such a laugh that we decided not to stop there.

We continued with our little game but changed the rules. Our road had about eighty houses in all. We knew that a few people in the neighbourhood didn't like each other, so we went from house to house, swapping neighbouring gates. Some neighbours had small wooden gates which we swapped with big metal ones. In those days it was simple to remove gates, as they fitted on two pins, unlike today, where they are welded onto their frames. We finally went home, exhausted from all the laughing and absolutely drained from lifting the gates. We passed out and slept deeply.

The next day, a huge commotion broke out in the street.

'What's going on?' I asked my mother, having completely forgotten about the night before.

'Somebody has swapped around all the gates in the neighbourhood,' she replied, eyeing me suspiciously. 'Do you know anything about this?'

I said no, of course, and, thank God, we weren't caught. It was a huge joke, but it had all been completely fruitless: sadly, the hot babe moved out of the brother-in-law's house soon afterwards.

I loved motor cars. The Three Musketeers needed one: we were cool and on the prowl for girls and parties. But none of us had the cash for our own car. Even though I had bought the Escort with my mother, she had more claim to it. In the mid 1970s, the most expensive car was the Chevrolet 2.500L, at R2 500; the cheapest was the Mini Minor, at R800. There were tons of VW Beetles around. When Michael, Luis and I waited to catch the bus to town, we often counted the number of Beetles passing by. I think they outnumbered the other cars on the road by ten to one.

In those days we could catch the bus and not worry about getting mugged. The worst we saw was some drunk trying to get home. We often used to hitch-hike or walk to town. On Saturdays we would go to the Wembley ice rink, about twenty kilometres away from our homes, although I never ever got the hang of skating. I was always too clumsy and kept falling over.

We often went to the rink to meet other friends. Life was

very different then. I think we had much more to do; there were no cellphones or home computers. We found many ways to entertain ourselves, spending a lot more time outdoors and not hunched up at a computer. But things have to change; I guess it's called progress.

And then, on Saturday nights, we'd go into Hillbrow. The place was always abuzz – the most cosmopolitan inner-city suburb in South Africa, with nightclubs, snooker dens, bookshops and tons of restaurants open pretty much twenty-four hours a day. We frequented one particular nightclub, Barbarello's, where live bands performed every night – one band that has stuck in my mind is Fantasy, which did a George Benson number called 'On Broadway'. You would've sworn that George himself was there. The crowds went mad. We had some good times in that place.

On Sundays we'd go to Café Wien, which had backgammon games and good coffee. Hillbrow was renowned for its record bars; the best one later became the first CD Warehouse. The owner, Lenny, always stocked the latest records long before anybody else did. On weekends when we didn't have the cash to hit Hillbrow, we played baseball in the park or back garden.

Many more of my friends were now receiving their call-up papers for military service. The war on the border was getting worse. Michael was called up and went off to fight in Angola after his basic training. For the first time, I was pleased to have Klinefelter's, since it had helped me escape the barbarism of the air force. I was still pretty naive politically and could not help being influenced by the state's brainwashing to promote its doctrine of fear.

I lived out the 1970s in a fog of work and play, but increasingly the political approached the personal. A cousin of mine was in the Special Forces. Rumours abounded about what was going on, but the government kept feeding us the story of having to prevent a 'Total Onslaught' from the communists. Of course it was the mantra all over the Western world – especially the USA, which was still in Vietnam. Little did we know that Angola was becoming *our* Vietnam.

My cousin was picked up in the dead of night to go and do whatever Special Forces do. He never spoke about what they got up to, but, as I've said, the rumours were rife – of infringements and atrocities and things no young men should do or see.

Michael came home on leave twice. He had become remote and quiet, unlike the gregarious, macho friend I had once known. He was also aggressive and didn't seem to like me much any more. I tried to talk to him, but he remained distant. I later learnt that he had survived two disastrous attacks. His platoon was ambushed deep in Angola, where the government denied the South African army had even been. He was the only survivor in one attack. Instead of telling stories of bravado and heroism, he growled and snarled at his old friends to keep us and the horrors in his mind away.

Then, in the mid- to late-1970s, South Africa started experiencing urban terrorism in the form of bombings. I was a few months into my printing apprenticeship. The company was situated in the middle of Johannesburg, in the shadow of the flyover near End and Durban streets. We were up on the third floor of an old, dingy building that was very gloomy inside. Half the time the lift didn't work – we had to slog up the stairs or use the goods lift. It still had an old steel grate that we had to pull across the doorway.

Often, travelling between home and work, I would wonder if a bomb might explode somewhere on my route. As I walked or rode past a car, I'd think, 'You never know when or where it'll happen next.'

One lunchtime, some work friends and I went to a local bar. We were about to have a few drinks when we suddenly heard a massive explosion. Running outside, we saw that a car bomb had gone off just a few feet away. Luckily, nobody was injured, but if we had arrived at that bar five minutes later, we would have been hit. That was the closest I came to experiencing urban terrorism in South Africa.

In 1976 the whole delusional bubble in which we had lived burst when the children of Soweto marched in protest against Afrikaans being the medium of instruction in their schools. The government reacted with violent force and police opened fire on innocent children. South Africa was plunged into chaos.

My family and I cocooned ourselves in the safety of our home, fearing what we didn't understand. I again felt relieved that I wasn't in the army, that I didn't have to go into Soweto and point a gun at little kids. I imagined being outside a house in the township, with Dolly or Agnes stepping out, and that I had to shoot at them. My parents, too, were ignorant of politics and were duped by the government propaganda.

Fear permeated the air. The government propaganda machine twisted the truth to make us fear the blacks, who were supposedly coming after us. Schools and colleges were on high alert; we believed that the whole of Soweto was coming to kill our students. One day at the tech, where I was taking classes, the liberal students of Wits University marched by.

The tech students went out to meet them, slinging insults: 'Commie!'

'Bloody Nats!' returned the Wits marchers.

The cops arrived and took the tech students' side.

And still the war on the border escalated. At home, my parents tried to distance themselves from what was happening around us. Every night on TV, the SABC announced the death of another soldier killed on the border.

I lost touch with Michael. Luis and I heard that he'd had another close shave, and had almost died this time. Boys we knew came back in body bags or, more frequently, mad. Young black men and women left the country in secret to enlist with the ANC in other African countries or went overseas to be trained by the Soviet military.

I never could understand why the Nationalist government suppressed black people. It didn't make sense to me, as a young person, but I was a product of my environment and never really questioned the status quo. In fact, I was just as much a fool as they were, because, when I turned eighteen, I voted for the National Party. It was either in innocence or utter stupidity, but, later on, when I saw what was going on, I changed my vote to the Progressive Party and had to take a lot of flak from my friends for doing so. I started keeping quiet about who received my vote.

17

Close calls

New Year's Eve in Johannesburg, 1979. I was now twenty-two years old and my life was about to change yet again. Four friends and I were looking forward to the night ahead, planning to attend every possible end-of-year party. I hoped to finish off the year with a bang.

We were all squashed into the tiny space of a Mini after leaving the last party. Enough revelling for one night: call it quits and head home. The seating plan had not changed all evening, but, for some reason (which I still wonder about), I wanted to move from the passenger seat to the back. There were three of us; I chose to sit in the middle, where I had more legroom.

We were singing at the top of our voices to the music on the cassette player, in the usual fashion of inebriated youths. Strangely enough, I have never forgotten the song playing on the tape – 'Feelings' – I think the artist was Morris Albert. I can still remember the lyrics: 'Feelings, nothing more than feelings ...'

The driver was more inebriated than we'd realised – not that any of us was in a position to point a finger – and he was probably going too fast. One minute we were on the road, the next the car was on the pavement. Telephone poles came hurtling towards us and I braced myself for impact. We all shouted, 'Stop!' but the car only travelled faster; the driver had panicked and stepped on the accelerator instead of the brake. The impact with the first pole wasn't too bad, though the pole snapped like a twig in the wind. For a moment we all thought this was rather amusing – it's amazing how alcohol can trick the brain. Hitting the first pole should have slowed the car down, but instead another pole loomed. The laughter in the car faded into a deathly silence – we might not be so lucky the next time round.

Our driver was still clinging desperately onto the steering wheel, but the speed of the car was not decreasing. The car hit the second pole, and suddenly everything became a blur as bodies were tossed around in the confined space. I heard someone crying out in pain – but who was it? The sound was coming from me. I felt an excruciating pain in my chest – as if I'd been hit with a ten-pound hammer. I blacked out – too much alcohol and too much pain.

What goes through one's mind in the last seconds of life? One moment I was seeing the telephone poles coming towards the car; the next I was standing behind the pole, watching the car hurtling towards me. I was entirely calm; I didn't feel fear or panic, or even apprehension, but it was strange watching myself. As the car hit the pole, I felt I had left the street. Then I flew back into the car and re-entered my physical body. As this happened, I grabbed onto the seat and braced myself so that I wouldn't be propelled through the windscreen. As my body hurtled forward, I expected the worst, but something stopped me – the gear stick was in my way.

My head hit the rear-view mirror, sending my glasses flying. Then a tingling sensation came over me and I felt myself drifting slowly upwards. I was floating – looking down on the car – and there was absolute quiet. I had what might be described as four-dimensional vision. I watched the car, as if in slow motion, and saw it collide with the second pole. It changed direction and stopped sideways, alongside a third pole.

Surrounding me was an incredibly beautiful white light, peace and tranquillity. I felt as if I had been in this space forever, and yet there wasn't any concept of time. Nothing seemed to matter. I didn't want to leave, to return to where I had come from.

Suddenly two people appeared next to me. I couldn't identify them, but I knew that I knew them and I felt safe. I somehow sensed that they were my guardian angels or guides. There was a female presence – a young girl – who looked very familiar. I'm sure she was my late sister Pamela, who had died a year before I was born. The other presence was a man, a very old man, with a long white beard. He seemed to be Chinese, perhaps Vietnamese. I felt I had known him for a long time and that I was totally safe. No words were necessary.

It was terrible to come back from such a beautiful space where the light was clear and bright and everything was calm. But I was not given a choice; nobody asked me if I wanted to stay, but then I suppose the Divine has its own plans.

And then my illusion was shattered.

The pain was back. What was going on? I wanted to be back in the beautiful, calm place. My body ached. I could smell petrol mixed with oil and the awful smell of vomit and blood. I struggled to breathe.

'Are we dead?' I wondered.

Suddenly Michael shouted, 'Quickly, get the fuck out! The car's on fire! It's going to explode!'

Panic-stricken, we scrambled out. The pain I felt when I moved was so intense that I would rather have gone up in flames with the car. But the will to survive was stronger, and I reached out my hand. We all crawled to a safe distance, only to see that the smoke of the 'fire' was the escaping steam of a smashed radiator.

From the sidelines we were able to assess the damage. The

car had come to a stop against the front wall of a house, without damaging the wall too much. The house's occupants had heard the collision and had come outside to investigate. We were all given sugar water to calm us down and taken to hospital.

Three of my friends had minor cuts and bruises. One also had a broken kneecap. The pain in my chest was caused by a broken sternum. Thank God the poles we had hit had been made of wood, not steel – our saving grace.

The doctors also picked up that my heart had stopped for a few moments during the accident, and they recommended that I spend the next few days under observation. They might have realised that I had had a near-death experience.

'Don't tell the police. Don't mention what you saw, and don't give a statement. Feign loss of memory. The cops will think you're off your rocker otherwise,' they advised.

I agreed, as I reckoned they probably knew what they were talking about.

The accident and the ensuing near-death experience was a turning point in my life. That moment of peace and light stayed with me for ages afterwards. I longed to go back to that state of bliss, to re-experience it. The guides had made me feel so safe and protected, and the experience started changing my outlook and beliefs, as well as my perspective. There was more to life than just being here on this planet. I began to see people, nature and events with new eyes.

Previously I hadn't *really* noticed what was going on in my immediate little world. Having a close shave is a wake-up call. I had had so many fears in my life: Was I going to have enough money? Would I be happy in my life or my marriage? And so on. Suddenly, whatever happened was not important any more, because it was beyond my control. I realised that there was something more, call it a superior being, call it whatever you like – God, Muhammad, Buddha or Jesus. It doesn't really matter. We are all part of the same universe; we are all part of God.

I started delving into different philosophies. Since I started thinking that death is just the beginning of many lives, my fear of dying and my doubts about where we all go when we die are not important any more. It is the most wonderful feeling to have. I live for the moment and don't focus on the future; I live each day as if it's my last. This way I don't get too many nasty surprises. I have also found that I am open to just about anything. Another thing this experience taught me is that I should always listen to my gut instinct. We all have it; it is like a direct message from God.

I've often wondered whether Pamela and the Asian man I saw are my guardian angels. As life moved on, I developed a sense of intuition. I became aware of warning bells ringing when I was in danger. I began thinking of Pamela and the man as my guides, a term I started using to refer to the people I perceive on the other side – the ones who have passed over. Some of them I can see, like Pamela. Others I merely sense are present. Sometimes I can feel that there are about five guides around me. In fact, I believe we all have our own guides.

After the accident, I began searching for answers: Why was I was on this planet? I had had so many close shaves, and sometimes death had seemed imminent. I wondered why I had survived. I started spending time in bookshops, reading books on the paranormal, on near-death experiences, on UFOs. Much has been written on these topics, but it was a subject most people didn't want to talk about (although these days it is not so taboo).

My mother and I spoke in depth about my near-death experience. She had always been inquisitive about other worlds and understood my soul-searching.

'Do you think Pamela could be my guardian angel?' I asked her.

'Yes,' she said. 'I often feel Pamela near me too.'

My mother had experienced many odd events in her life. She never scoffed at the paranormal. We discussed whether we earthlings are the only people in the universe. My feeling was that there are about as many different creatures in other solar systems as there are on earth.

As my mother was growing old, we often spoke about death. She said she wished she knew more about it. I tried to reassure her, saying, 'It all works out,' but she often thought otherwise. Some of our most interesting conversations were about health – a passion we both shared. As I've said, she always regretted giving up nursing. We would talk for hours about our views on various illnesses and what caused them, and about doctors who were so often arrogant and closed to alternative explanations.

Over the years, many people have said that I have very strange ideas – that the way I see the world is somewhat different from the normal point of view. Perhaps this is the case because I am fortunate enough to have crossed the threshold and returned.

PART THREE

Of bones, stones and endings

18

A marriage and a sperm count

I was now a qualified printer and there were several different areas I could choose to specialise in: platemaking, compositing, photo-lithography, stripping, proofreading, guillotine operating and machine-minding.

The whole process started with the compositor. Clients brought along a document or a pamphlet they wanted printed. It was given to the compositor, who would type up the text and insert any graphics. It was then scanned by the photo-lithographers. In turn, the material was stripped into film or, as in the old days, cast into lead slugs. After the material was made up, it was sent over to the proofreaders for correction. Only then could the platemakers place it on an aluminium plate and burn an image from the film. It would normally be exposed to ultraviolet light for about three minutes.

The platemaker then took the plate to a trough, poured chemicals over it and allowed the images to develop. Once dry, the plates came to the machine-minders: this was the position I had chosen. My role was to set up the machine and make sure that the paper went through it smoothly and that the ink ducts were set correctly. I was responsible for the final product.

Once the images were printed and the ink was dry, the job went to the guillotine operators to be cut. Then it was wrapped and packed, ready for delivery. This process could take anything from a couple of days to two weeks.

In the meantime, time ticked on. I enjoyed my job as a

machine-minder – it was a practical position and I felt in control of it.

Then, in 1982, I met Marina at a mutual friend's house, and I was attracted to her immediately. She had a great sense of humour, and gave as good as she got – she was quite cocky. I liked this in a woman – a daring side to her. I hadn't really had any girlfriends since Theresa; just casual dates.

Marina agreed to go on a date with me a few days later. We had a great time, laughing and chatting, and we felt relaxed in each other's company. Shortly afterwards we went to the movies and, later that week, to dinner. We continued to get on well: we joked about the same things and shared many laughs.

I was still a virgin and also still had many complexes about my sexual ability and the size of my penis. I had no way of knowing whether I was normal or if I could perform sexually. But I believed I was ready to have a go at a real relationship. Marina and I started to date seriously. She was lovely, with long dark hair and big brown eyes. Soon, I was in love. Marina was born in Cyprus but had spent most of her life in South Africa, her parents having emigrated eighteen years previously.

Our relationship moved swiftly towards the bedroom. We actually made our first tentative love on the back seat of a car. I had fantasised about the moment for so long, and I was both nervous and excited. But my feelings of inadequacy were lying close to the surface and I feared I would not be man enough *or* big enough.

Marina was a virgin too, but she encouraged me and we fumbled along. I had dabbled around, had oral sex, but I had never had intercourse with anybody. I was twenty-two years old. I found that it was very difficult for Marina to have sex for the first time; I think the first time must be difficult for any woman. It was very painful for Marina when I tried to penetrate her, so I had to be patient. The last thing I wanted was for her to have a bad first experience. And I was just as inexperienced as she was!

Having intercourse wasn't physically painful for me; rather, it was more painful mentally. I was feeling very frustrated, but after a couple of weeks we finally managed to get it right. I had watched porn flicks, or blue movies, at a friend's house when I was younger and had an idea of what I wanted, but I was also game to experiment. Marina, on the other hand, was very naive. So, when I suggested certain positions, she reacted with horror. With some reassurance, she soon relaxed. I didn't believe in forcing anything on her; everything would happen in its own time. I was also scared of an unwanted pregnancy, as many of my male friends had had one-night stands during which the girls had fallen pregnant because they hadn't taken precautions.

Marina came from a Greek Orthodox family and we both feared her falling pregnant. I did not have ready access to any condoms and she had never been on the pill. We should definitely have taken precautions, but contraception was tricky in those days. I would have had to go to the chemist and ask for condoms at the counter, which would have been so embarrassing, as the condoms were kept in a drawer behind the till and the shop assistant was a strict, headmistress-like woman.

Marina said she could get the pill only from her doctor, who needed her mother's permission to prescribe it to her. We were both afraid and inexperienced, and so, when we had sex, I would pull out before ejaculating. If only I'd known then ... But we found our way, fumbling around, until we had done the deed. And it was fine! We both enjoyed it and Marina assured me that I was a good lover.

One day Marina and I drove into town to browse around and have coffee. A friend of hers imported jewellery from Israel and ran a shop in Eloff Street that was much cheaper than other jewellers. Marina suggested we go and have a look at the jewellery. 'No harm,' I thought, but, looking back, I am sure she'd had a plan.

We parked at the local parkade and made our way to the shop, on the tenth floor, where we rang the buzzer. Marina's friend let us in and asked if there was anything we were particularly interested in seeing. Marina asked to have a look at the diamond rings. I thought this was rather odd, but decided to indulge her.

The jeweller placed a tray of assorted rings in front of us. Marina picked up a few, tried them on and said, 'What do you think?' What was I supposed to say? I wanted to get married sometime in my life, but I wasn't sure that I wanted it right then. I suppose she gave me a little push – in fact, more like a shove. For the next couple of weeks, she kept asking me if I wanted to get married and have children. I said I did, but pretty much left it there.

One day, talking about marriage again, she asked, 'What about us?'

After another week or so, one day I just said, 'Okay, let's get married.'

I think deciding to get married was a combination of Marina wanting to leave home and me being pressured by her and our friends. I was also tired of sex in cars and at friends' places. I wanted to have my own place and not feel any guilt.

So, after going out for four years, we decided to get married. I had to ask her parents for their daughter's hand. They were a traditional Greek family who made a living in the restaurant trade. Although I got on well with Marina's parents and felt that they accepted me, approaching my future father-in-law took a lot of courage and nerve, and Marina and I discussed how to go about it beforehand.

'Don't worry,' she reassured me. 'My dad will be cool about this.'

That evening I went to her parents' home, arriving just after supper. I entered the house, greeted her brother Nick and younger sister Debbie, and walked into the kitchen. The family often had supper at the kitchen table. I could feel my hands starting to sweat. My stomach felt tight and perspiration was forming on my upper lip. I knew I needed to do this as quickly as possible or my courage would fail me. At first we made small talk, and then I just blurted it out: I told her father that I wanted to marry his daughter.

There was absolute silence for a moment. He looked at me and then quickly across at Marina's mother and then back at me. The proposal had probably come as a bit of a shock to him. I don't think he and Marina's mother had expected our relationship to last, and they would probably have preferred a Greek son-in-law. I was about to say sorry, I had made a mistake, when he suddenly said, 'That's wonderful!'

My soon-to-be father-in-law got up and grabbed me, and gave me a firm hug. Then he kissed me on both cheeks and patted me on the back, in real Greek fashion, *thump! thump!* Was he just pretending? We'd had our differences, primarily cultural differences, but this had been so easy! Marina grinned.

Her mom and dad smiled. They brought out wine for a celebratory drink. I was flabbergasted. Could it be so simple?

The big day was planned for June 1984. South African law did not recognise a marriage in the Greek Orthodox Church, so we had to bring our plans forward for a civil marriage in February 1984.

But then, in December 1983, disaster struck Marina's family. Debbie, who had had problems both at home and at school, took recreational drugs. At the time, her parents had relatives staying with them, one of whom carried a gun for protection. Debbie found the gun where it had been left in a cupboard and went downstairs to the kitchen.

She sat down at the table, still holding the gun, but got no response from the family until she threatened to shoot herself. As her parents jumped up screaming, Debbie squeezed the trigger and the bullet ripped through her aorta, leaving her dead within moments. Her parents, of course, were traumatised; her life had ended at the tender age of sixteen. The police found that Debbie had emptied the gun of its magazine (which they found upstairs), but a stray bullet had been left in the chamber. I wonder if Debbie would have pulled the trigger had she known about the bullet. She was depressed at the time – was she trying to get her parents' attention by scaring them?

The family was numb with shock, but Marina and I decided to go ahead with our wedding plans. During this time, I got to know the family a little better. Marina and I often had meals with them to give them comfort after Debbie's death. They seemed happy with the impending wedding. But others around me were worried.

One night our family doctor asked me to pop around for a little chat.

'What is this about?' I wondered. 'Perhaps he wants me to visit him so he can play the role of a counsellor or a priest – offer a little bit of marriage guidance?'

He asked me straight out: 'How long have you been dating this woman?' I thought it a strange question.

'What do you really want to talk to me about?' I asked.

I watched him as he talked – his mouth was moving – but I didn't hear a word; or, rather, I didn't *want* to hear a word. I was in shock – had I heard correctly?

'You need to go to the fertility clinic to check whether you can father children.'

According to statistics, men with Klinefelter's syndrome have an extremely low sperm count. In most cases, they are infertile. My chances of fathering a child were pretty much non-existent, my doctor told me. Adult xxy males are not able to manufacture sufficient sperm to father children – although there have been a few exceptions. Although adult xxy males are usually capable of normal erection and ejaculation, the sperm count is very low due to the underdevelopment of the testicles.

Now I understood his question. How was I ever going to break this to Marina, just a few months before our wedding? Why hadn't I been told earlier, when I was seventeen and undergoing those treatments? I was in a daze and also very confused. My mind was numb as I drove to the fertility clinic.

I was deeply troubled by the news: I hadn't even got married yet, and already there was an obstacle in my path. In the back of my mind I already knew what the result of the test would be. But why would the doctor break the news at this stage?

Maybe he thought that I was having second thoughts, wondering whether I was doing the right thing? I was wondering too. All my friends were getting married, but I wasn't certain if that was what I wanted.

The consulting rooms were exactly as they appear in the movies. I felt as though the whole world was watching me. It was terribly disconcerting. Ice-cold fear and dread crept, snake-like, up my legs. My stomach churned and all at once I felt very queasy. I wanted to make a run for it, but my legs had turned to lead and fear held me ensnared. I sat mutely, as if I was back at the endocrinologist, sixteen again.

I was overcome with apprehension and rampant emotion. Then I suddenly numbed out. It was as if my mother was there with me, saying, 'Go ahead and don't complain. This is for the best.'

I suddenly felt very angry. I suppose she was doing her best at the time; the situation wasn't her fault. *She* wasn't the problem. Marina wasn't the problem. *I* was the problem.

I jumped as the receptionist suddenly appeared in front of me, handing me some forms to fill in. I filled them out like an automaton and then waited my turn. Eventually a female nurse escorted me to a cubicle and handed me a test tube: a small quantity would be enough for the test to be done. There were a few well-worn pornographic magazines at hand, but I felt no excitement at the prospect. I looked around the room for hidden cameras – it's amazing what goes through one's mind.

I hated the place with a sudden fury. I wanted to beat down the door and run out of the room. But I sat there like a stone, feeling the same numbing fear choking up my throat. I stared at the magazines in my hand. What I was now expected to do was too much: I got up, threw the magazine down and stormed out. The nurse looked up in surprise, but I just left her there, left them all and left the dreaded place.

When I got home, I locked the door of my room and flung myself on the bed. Feelings seemed to come from under the bed, from outside, flooding through the windows: I was overwhelmed with anger and shame. I lay and cried until I felt as if I were drowning in sweat and tears.

After a long time I sat up and managed to compose myself, wondering what had just happened to me. Drained and exhausted, I made myself a cup of tea and went to sit on the patio so that I could stare into the night sky. Slowly, I came back to myself. I knew that, deep down, I had stored away the memory of the endocrinologist's abuse. I hadn't thought about it for years, but the visit to the doctor and what I had been expected to do brought it all flooding back.

I managed to calm down by telling myself that I would fill a tube in my own good time. Later I called the doctor and told him I would bring in a fresh sample in a few days. He agreed. About three days later, I managed to fill an empty film spool container. I had to steer my mind away from thoughts of what had happened in the past in order to get the job done: both the outside pressures and my own self-consciousness made it take much longer than one would have expected.

'We'll contact you when we have the results,' they said at the doctor's when I handed in the little tube.

It was like awaiting a death sentence.

I didn't tell Marina about my experience or the flashbacks. I just told her that I had handed in a sample.

'All will be fine, you'll see,' she said reassuringly.

A few evenings later we had dinner with my sister and her husband. I told Christine about the sperm tests and we discussed the possibility that I might be sterile. Christine kept emphasising to Marina, 'Don't go through with the marriage if you feel that Stephen's sterility is going to be a problem.'

The days dragged on. Finally, the results.

Sterile.

The sperm count did not even add up to one per cent. Nothing could be done about it. Although it was nobody else's business but mine and Marina's, I went home and called Christine. She was shocked, but tried to reassure me that this would not be an issue in my relationship.

Although the possibility that I might be sterile had concerned me before, I was now certain. I felt I had failed Marina. She would never bear my children. Should I cancel the wedding? I went over to Marina's house with the news. She was standing over the stove, cooking a meal for the family. She looked over at me with the mixing spoon suspended in mid-air. She didn't say a word; I am sure my face told the story. I felt that my world had come to an end.

But Marina assured me that she loved me, regardless. We had two options: adoption or artificial insemination. Neither of these was a problem to her, nor was the fact that I would never be able to father children. And so our relationship continued as before, and we even managed to keep our secret to ourselves.

But the following months were not happy ones. Marina and I began to argue over trivial matters. We should have postponed the wedding, but already the wheels were in motion. I thought the event might bring a little joy to her family, who were still grieving the loss of their daughter and sister, but there was a lot of pressure after the suicide. Suddenly everything became an uphill battle.

I couldn't concentrate at work; I was making silly mistakes. Things that normally would not have been a problem became overwhelming. I became edgy, jumpy, reacting to the smallest of triggers. My confidence slowly waned, and my complexes crushed me.

Marina couldn't understand it. She wanted to make love, but I found every excuse to avoid it. Our arguments became more frequent. Marina accused me of not considering her feelings regarding her sister's death. Apparently I didn't give a damn about how she was feeling, as I was too self-absorbed – concerned and upset only with the thought that I could not have children.

But it was the memories of the doctor's abuse that kept infiltrating my thoughts. When I closed my eyes at night, a screen unfurled in my head and I watched the events as a slide show: me at the doctor's door; me going in to sit on the side of the bed; him towering above me, telling me to take off my clothes; me lying there naked; his smirking eyes; his hand running up and down my little penis; my eyes rolling back to hide from it all; his invasive questions.

Whereas I'd blocked the recollection of being sexually abused for a long time, now the memory of it hit me. It was as if I was reliving the entire experience. Only this time, I understood that I was being abused.

Marina's mother also became a problem. Her despair was apparent and it seemed to draw me in every time I looked into her dark-brown eyes. It made me feel small, like a thirteen-year-old. How could I ever please her daughter? Marina also felt the pressure from her mother, who was demanding and teary, always asking Marina to stay with her in the evenings. I understood that, following the death of Debbie, they were both under strain. But I had doubts and I feared for the future.

I wasn't sure any more that I wanted to get married. My insecurities were too overwhelming. Would Marina still love me when she desired children in the future? Also, our arguments had shown me a very different side to my future wife; she often acted like a spoilt brat, demanding attention. Although my own insecurities and inadequacies appalled me, I found Marina's behaviour unbearable at times.

I think something had died inside all of us on the fateful night Debbie shot herself. Both Marina and I were behaving badly. I started to have serious doubts about wanting to spend the rest of my life with this person. Maybe she had always been like this, and I had chosen to ignore it, as we all do when in love. Suddenly I was certain I didn't want to go down this road: my gut instinct was telling me to walk away. But I chose not to listen. I should have called the wedding off, but I was deeply concerned that Marina's parents might think me insensitive after Debbie's death.

And so the wedding went ahead – Marina and I just went along with it. A few months prior to the event, I started working for a new company that printed calendars, and I worked to strict deadlines. The timing of our wedding was unfortunate all round.

Some of Marina's relations in Cyprus wanted to see us, so we planned our honeymoon around a trip to the island to accommodate their wishes. Our plan was to leave eighteen months after the wedding, when the family would all be there.

Marina and I were still arguing, and most of our disagreements were about her late sister – I was accused of not being supportive enough of Marina. In turn, she didn't understand my feelings of inadequacy.

Our honeymoon was planned to start in Spain, after which we would visit Italy. Although we had wanted the trip – we chose the destinations and a travel agent booked our hotels – we did not enjoy it. For six weeks, we fought like cat and dog. I was quite happy not to spend a lot of money on fancy hotels. I would have been satisfied with a pensione or B&B, but Marina believed such accommodation was beneath her and that we should treat ourselves. She wanted her honeymoon to be in the most expensive hotels, saying we would just use our credit cards (that little exercise took eighteen months to pay off).

We stayed in Madrid for two days and then flew to the Costa del Sol on the south coast of Spain. The four days there were a revelation to me. It was 1984, a year before the major political protests would start in South Africa. At the hotel, the desk clerk asked for our passports – standard procedure for visitors – and we went to our rooms to freshen up. A few hours later we came down for dinner and some entertainment. A stand-up comedian from England was telling jokes, and he eventually asked members of the audience where they were from. When the microphone was handed to us, we said, 'South Africa.' Booing ensued from the other hotel visitors, most of whom were from either Holland or Germany.

The comedian quickly took the situation in hand, telling the audience he had performed in Cape Town and that South Africa was a very beautiful country. However, some people sitting next to us moved away and the next day, in the lobby, people glared at us and muttered under their breath.

Our next stop was Rome, from where we flew to Greece. Owing to an error by the travel agent, instead of connecting to Paphos, we had no choice but to wait ten hours for a flight to Limassol. Marina said we should book into a hotel for the duration. I said she must be mad, instead suggesting that we go and have lunch somewhere, do a bit of shopping and then return to the airport.

Not a chance. I now had the opportunity to see how Marina could sulk if she didn't get her own way. Of course she won. We spent the rest of the day in a hotel room.

Late that evening we caught a flight to Cyprus, where I finally met the extended family – the old *yayas* ('grannies' in Greek) and Marina's uncles and aunts. They lived a sheltered life on the island. Marina and I had been sexually active for the previous five years but we encountered a problem when we got to Cyprus: the *yayas* put us into single beds in the same room.

'Hasn't anybody told them we're married?' I wondered. 'Married people sleep in the same bed. I mean, we aren't going to bring down the village roof.' For the next two weeks, we sneaked around like two teenagers, getting a bit of nooky here and there, but, as we fought more and more, the sex seemed to take a back seat.

In those days the international media presented South Africa in a very negative light. One night, I watched a TV report that had cleverly spliced together a scene of policemen on horseback shooting people in Eloff Street, Johannesburg. I recognised the place by the familiar statue of the springboks jumping over the fountain.

The family in Cyprus, concerned for our safety, decided South Africa was no longer safe and that we were to remain in Cyprus – permanently. This took me completely by surprise. There had been no discussions with either Marina or her family. Marina was happy to stay. I had to fight the whole lot – it took some effort to convince them that I had to go home to get my affairs in order. Looking back, it felt as if I had a role in the film *Not without My Daughter*.

We managed to get away eventually; Christine was holidaying on Mykonos, and we told Marina's family that we were going to see her, pretending we would return. But we took our luggage and passports along and, after visiting Christine, headed back to South Africa.

Back home, our relationship did not improve. The fighting continued. In hindsight, I believe couples should live together before marrying, so that they can get to know each other more intimately. We didn't have the benefit of such experience.

When my wife saw something she liked, she wanted it immediately; I would have preferred to buy it when we could afford it. On one occasion, a wall unit she wanted for our hi-fi caught her attention. I said I would put in a bit of overtime and we would buy it at the end of the month. That was far too long for her to wait.

'I'll speak to my father,' she said, 'and he can help us.'

I tried to argue, but she wasn't having any of it. In anger, I eventually left our flat and drove around for a while. A few days later, as I was arriving home from work, I saw men from the Hypermarket delivering a wall unit. I told them that they must have the wrong address, but they insisted they were at the right place. To make sure, I checked the name at the bottom of the sheet of paper – her father's. I couldn't believe it. Here I was, working my butt off every night to buy this unit, but my wife couldn't wait. She had to have it now. We argued again, and then she sulked.

Marina could sulk for weeks at a time, and then there was no communication between us at all. When she wasn't sulking, we argued constantly, and during our arguments my sterility was thrown in my face. According to her, I was not 'man enough'. The marriage came to an end six months after our honeymoon. We had been married for two years. I do not lay all the blame on her – we were both immature and had had a lot to deal with in a short time.

We separated prior to getting divorced. It was with a sense of great relief that I walked away, knowing that it was all over. I had come to realise that I no longer loved her. However, for a while I still had to endure her company. Johnny's wife, Val, insisted on inviting Marina to all our family occasions. It hurt to see her there – all the stuff that had happened stood like an elephant between us. Christine also kept on inviting her over – they were friends, and Christine wanted to show Marina that the divorce hadn't been all her fault. Of course it hadn't. I knew that, but it still hurt.

19

Martial arts and fragile bones

I was alone again, living in a flat in Johannesburg, trying to rebuild my life. I continued practising martial arts, something that had always given me great pleasure. I'd been involved with martial arts since my late high school years and I especially loved karate. It was the only sport I really enjoyed; it gave me confidence. Like with most things in life, it had a downside though – I broke the odd rib and even the occasional finger. The doctors didn't think the broken bones were anything strange, and presumably put it down to training partners who punched and kicked too hard. I continued to enjoy my practice sessions and eventually progressed to black-belt level (first dan).

I was almost due for a karate evaluation, but about six months prior to the evaluation, I caught a guy hanging about suspiciously near my car. Alarm bells rang: his dirty denims and T-shirt hung loosely on his tall, lanky frame (he was a good six foot four), and his large, menacing eyes protruded strangely from their sockets. I soon realised that he was breaking into my vehicle. In my martial arts class, we had talked about how we would react if such an event occurred – we would act our meanest. Well, reality is not like the movies. Everything I'd learnt went out the window; I was scared.

When the man saw me, he jumped away from the car and pulled out a huge knife. 'Shit, what do I do now?' I thought. 'I wasn't taught how to handle this.' I was trying to jump out of his way when I realised that he was as scared as I was, which could be even more dangerous. I was fearing for my life but trying to calm him down at the same time. A thought flashed through my mind: 'Does he have accomplices hiding in the bushes?'

Fortunately for me, the knifeman ran off into the park. Besides shaking like a leaf, I had come out of the incident unscathed, but it unsettled me and made me look differently at my favourite sport. After seven years of training, I had been unable to defend myself effectively against an attacker with a knife. The karate class did not teach that. The next day I told the dojo I was quitting.

I still had a love for martial arts and started looking for another form that would be of more benefit to me, should I ever find myself in a similar situation. I found a school that taught ju-jitsu. This form teaches one to go at attackers, regardless of their size, using their body weight to their disadvantage. Unlike karate, where one has to rely on strength and muscle to knock an opponent down, ju-jitsu teaches one to deflect attacks. It also enables one to defend oneself against knife attacks. I learnt the pressure points, strangleholds and how to immobilise an opponent.

Ju-jitsu came naturally to me, probably because of my years of doing karate. I practised the sport for about eighteen months, moving up the ranks at a steady pace, and attained my green belt. I was pretty happy with life in general, but, as usual, the comfort zone didn't last very long.

It was 1988 and I was enjoying a ju-jitsu class. I was going through the motions and was about to execute a well-practised move. I had an opponent named Ian by the arm and was about to throw him over my shoulder when he said, 'The move feels wrong.'

I contradicted him: 'It's fine.'

Then, in a split second, the throw – an over-the-shoulder movement – went wrong. Instead of going over the top of my shoulder, he went around the side, landing on my knee. We both crashed to the ground. Excruciating pain immediately shot through my knee. I couldn't move. My knee felt as if it had popped out of its joint.

I eventually managed to stand up, but with great difficulty. Everybody was concerned, but after a little rest I said, 'Don't worry guys, everything will be okay.'

I drove home, struggling considerably with the clutch. I didn't ascribe the problem to the knee – I thought it must be the car. By the time I got into bed, I had to resort to painkillers and hope that by morning all would be well. Not so. The pain was worse.

My GP referred me to an orthopaedic surgeon: 'One of the best,' he said.

The surgeon examined my knee. 'We need to operate,' he said. 'The ligament is torn off the kneecap. It's a simple procedure.'

He assured me I would only be in hospital for two days and back at work after a week.

A little voice inside my head whispered, 'Get a second opinion.'

But how often do we listen to our inner voices? I had given my guides the afternoon off. What did I know about knee surgery?

I was booked in the following day, and so began another major chapter in my life.

I tried hard to relax as I was admitted to theatre, all prepared for the operation. The anaesthetist tried to reassure me as I went under. When I woke up some hours later, I felt a terrible pain throughout my body. I presumed it was the after-effects of surgery. I was in a plaster cast from hip to toe, with my leg hoisted above the bed. On his rounds, the surgeon repeated that I would be in hospital for two days, but the pain led me to believe that I'd be in bed for the next year. I received morphine every six hours.

'Why is there so much pain?' I asked.

The doctor explained that, in order to stabilise the knee, they had inserted two pins. The damage to the knee was worse than they had anticipated. Was this to be the end of my ju-jitsu sessions?

The doctor assured me that my injury was not serious – just a torn ligament. But still he made no mention of the damage to the knee. I was once more reassured with: 'Everything will be all right. Don't worry.'

Easy for him to say – it was not his leg. Again my gut started talking: something was amiss here. But my hands (or my leg in this case) were tied.

Then the surgeon took two weeks' leave. Each time the locum did his daily rounds, he admonished me, 'Make an effort. Get up. Move around.'

I got the same from the nurses every day too. Believe me, I wanted to – I wanted to go home. But my efforts diminished; the pain was unbearable. I told the doctor, who responded, 'It's all in your head. There is no pain.'

Maybe this is a standard phrase they were taught at medical school. Didn't the course cover bedside manner and empathy?

Two days ran into a couple of weeks. I still could not get out of bed. The humiliation of the bedpan had long dissipated. Each time I tried to stand, a nurse had to massage my backside, as it had 'gone to sleep'.

The pain ran through my body like an electric shock; it pulsated whenever the morphine wore off. A week into my stay, a locum insisted I get out of bed and stop feeling sorry for myself. Had this man ever suffered any pain from surgery? Again I was told it was all in my head. The locum was standing at the ward door. In a voice that sounded like he had spent time in the military, he ordered me out of bed.

I obeyed. I swung myself out of the bed, and, though I wanted to die from the pain, made my way towards him. I hobbled, just short of falling over.

He again said, 'You're imagining the pain.'

Something in my brain snapped. I lunged towards the idiot, grabbed him by the collar and began to drag him towards the window. He was going to fly through it – that would shut him up for good. And I'd go out with him – at least that would stop the pain.

The man screamed for help, and two male nurses (or should I say thugs?) arrived and struggled to loosen my grip on the idiot. How strong one is once one's temper has snapped and the adrenalin is pumping! Although the window did not break, the glass was buckling outwards – but I didn't have the strength to push him out.

Someone shouted, 'Sedate him!' I felt the needle jab in my arm – no immediate effect.

The doctor screamed, 'Another jab!' It came within seconds of the last.

Before I finally let go and sank into oblivion, I heard the nurse say, 'Another shot will probably kill him.'

The doctor spat out, 'I don't care.'

I woke up eight hours later to see my mother sitting next to my bed.

'You caused a huge commotion,' she said. 'The doctor wants to lay an assault charge against you.'

I wondered what charge I could lay against him. Mental abuse? I wished I could have him sent to a Gulag in Siberia for a year.

However, the doctor and I agreed that no charges would be laid. My own surgeon returned a few days later. Too bad – he had missed all the action. He cut off the plaster cast, only to discover that the stitches had caught on the cotton wool inside. Every time I stretched my leg, the stitches pulled. My leg was encased in a new cast and I lay in bed for a further two weeks. Boy, was I glad to see the back of that hospital in the end (and I am sure the feeling was mutual).

I struggled with my life in plaster for a week. The pain returned. More tests diagnosed a thrombosis in my leg, so back I went to the hospital. The gods were not on my side. The surgeon removed the cast, drained the thrombosis by inserting a needle into my foot, and reapplied plaster.

I had been living in my own flat for about two years. With a leg in plaster I could still make a cup of coffee, but I had to stand and drink it in the kitchen, as I needed both hands for the crutches. Bathing myself was a nightmare.

My parents had suggested I come back to live with them until I found my feet, so to speak. I was in my late twenties, and I had vowed never to go back home. I suppose I was fortunate that my parents could extend their hospitality and lend a hand in the process. The decision was eventually forced on me when I nearly drowned in six inches of water one night.

The cast ran from my toes to my hip; the hospital had also fixed a piece of rubber at the base of the plaster to act as a non-slip sole. In order to bath, I had to lie on my side and keep the plastered leg raised. It was extremely difficult, but at least I could feel the wonderful warm water touching my body. In the hospital, the nurses had washed me in bed. I had longed to lie in a bath and feel water lapping over me, as I did now.

When the water started to get cold, I reached over to the taps. It was quite an effort, but having long arms helped. The next thing I knew, the leg in plaster had slipped into the bath – its sheer weight had caught me off balance. I flipped over onto my good side, trying to cushion my leg, and my head dipped under the water. Although I tried, the weight of the plaster and the position I was in made it impossible for me to lift my head above the water. I knew I would have only seconds before I drowned. My mind was racing. The only escape was to try to pull the plug out.

'Don't panic,' I kept telling myself.

I grabbed the chain attached to the plug with my foot to try to yank it out. I tugged and tugged for what seemed like minutes, but it must have been only seconds before I heard the gurgle of the water going down the drain. Another two long seconds before I could take in some air ... I lay there gasping until I had gathered enough strength to pull myself upwards and spin my body around. I grabbed the side of the bath with both hands and lifted myself out.

'I need help,' I said, and made up my mind to go home then and there.

The next day I phoned my cousin Desmond, asking for a lift to my parents' house. Now the thought of moving in with them was a relief. Things got a bit awkward when I had to ask my father to help me wash, though. At first it was embarrassing, but after a while I just accepted the reality of the situation. Fortunately my father was in one of his great, fun moods, so he was helpful and often made light of things.

I slept in the dining room on a single bed against the wall, as my mother was still letting rooms out to boarders. Dave, a personal friend of ours, was renting one room in the house at the time. Sleeping in the dining room meant I couldn't sleep late or nap if visitors arrived, but living at home wasn't too bad overall.

Near the end of my three-month stay, my father's mood started to change for the worse. He often couldn't remember that I was divorced. He'd ask ten times a day, 'Where is Marina?' and 'Why are you staying with us?'

I also had to listen to my mother shouting at him at all hours of the night: 'Stop snoring, Johnny!' or 'Where are you going now, Johnny?'

Finally the plaster was removed and I could move around a lot more freely. I started to drive again, and relished not having to ask people for lifts.

During this stage of my life, I asked myself regularly what lesson I had not yet learnt. It was one of the most difficult periods of my life. I had to deal with the cock-up the surgeon had made, being off work for three months and relearning how to walk.

At that time I didn't fully understand the effects of testosterone. When the doctors first took me off the monthly injections, my self-confidence and self-esteem plummeted. Karate helped to restore some confidence. However, I had no idea then that my bones were weak because my body was not producing its own testosterone. I most likely already had the beginnings of osteoporosis – a side effect of Klinefelter's syndrome. This would explain why my bones always broke so easily. But at the time I didn't know that. After I'd struggled around for months, the surgeon removed the pins. I sighed: 'At last this is all over. I can move on with my life.'

The doctors suggested I undergo physiotherapy, which sounded very nice – or rather, the massage aspect of it. But as for the rest? It was a hard slog. I had to learn how to walk again, lifting weights and manoeuvring my leg around every day. During the electrotherapy, a new pain emerged – a shock-like stab.

'Something doesn't seem right here,' the physiotherapist said. 'I think you should go back and see the surgeon.'

Before I did that, I met Janine. It happened like this: Kenny, a new friend, and I went to a pub in Rockey Street in Yeoville. I had just had the cast removed from my knee after three months and was relying heavily on the crutches – I had also lost a lot of weight and my muscles were still weak. As we tried to enter the pub, some people were blocking the doorway. There were two men and a woman, and the men started joking about my gammy leg. I grinned sheepishly. Then the woman stepped forward.

'We have a knee in common,' she said.

I looked over my shoulder, not certain she was talking to me, but then replied, 'I injured myself doing ju-jitsu.'

'What happened?' she asked. She introduced herself as

Janine and seemed concerned and caring. I told her my sorry saga and how the doctors had had to repair the ligaments.

'I also hurt my knee,' she told me. We chatted about knee surgery for the next couple of minutes. I told her my surgeon had really messed up my knee.

'Who did your surgery?' she enquired.

'Doctor Shitface,' I replied, frustrated with how I could not name doctors for fear of being sued. We laughed at our shared experiences, enjoying each other's company. Then her friends got agitated, saying it was time to go.

'Why not see the surgeon who operated on my knee?' Janine suggested.

'Can I see you again?' I asked.

'That would be great,' she answered, giving me her number.

Not thinking anything would come of it, but deciding to give it a try, I called her a few days later. She gave me her surgeon's number and then agreed to a date. I made an appointment with Janine's surgeon the very next day.

'Why did the surgeon cut so deeply?' the new guy asked when he examined the knee.

After taking X-rays he studied them, and his face gave his thoughts away.

'Oh dear,' he said. 'We have a problem.'

A foreign object – a washer – was lodged in my knee, and the bone had grown around it. Another operation was necessary. This was supposedly a simple procedure, but it took six trips to the hospital and the physiotherapy would continue for nearly a year. It would be many months before I could walk properly again.

A year later, I tried to file a malpractice suit against the surgeon – but South Africa is protective of its doctors. The expense was a problem for me, as the costs would not be waived. My medical aid had long since dried up and this incident had already cost me thousands. I only wish that I had seen Janine's surgeon the first time.

Janine and I had been going out for about a month when the time came for the 'I can't father children' bit, before we got too involved. I tried to choose the right moment to broach the subject; I thought the best time would be over dinner, so I made reservations at a good restaurant. While we were having a laugh about something, I decided it was now or never.

'Janine, I need to talk to you about something,' I started nervously.

'You look very serious,' she said. 'Is everything okay?'

I could feel my hands starting to sweat and a tight knot forming in my stomach.

'I cannot have any children; I am sterile,' I blurted out. I waited for her shocked reaction, but she just went quiet for a while.

'When did you find out about this?' she asked.

I told her about Marina and that I had had myself checked out just before we got married. 'It was one of the reasons Marina divorced me,' I told her.

'We can always adopt,' she said at last.

In fact, she didn't seem fazed at all. A year later we were engaged.

20

Ignoring gut feelings

Before I met Janine, I was re-employed by the printing firm at which I had done my apprenticeship. I had left it for another company for four years, and had declined a previous offer to return. I felt it wasn't a good idea to go back to a company once you had left it.

I should have listened to that gut feeling, but I didn't. The firm came back with a counter-offer I couldn't refuse. A week later, I was back working at the firm in its new location, an industrial area in Denver, on the eastern outskirts of Johannesburg.

It was at this time that I met Kenny. We had both recently been divorced; we found common ground and became friends. One of Kenny's stories should have rung warning bells. He told me that he had been a 'guest' at Sterkfontein – the state hospital for the mentally ill. But I have always believed in giving people a fair chance, and besides, the state could have been wrong about Kenny. He was a nice enough guy. An ex-policeman, he told me he had had a small disagreement with some of his colleagues, after which 'a little shoot-out' had ensued. The result was that he had been committed to Sterkfontein hospital.

Just two days before Christmas, in 1989, I was alone at home one evening. Janine was working at a car rental business at the airport; shift work was part of her life. Kenny phoned from Sandton.

'I'm in trouble,' he said. 'A couple of guys are at my house. They're going to fuck me up.'

I was still recovering from the knee op. I still had a limp and supported myself on one crutch, but I felt I had to help my friend. Also, he insisted. Perhaps I could negotiate with these guys? He gave me the address.

'Tell no one where you are going,' Kenny said. Something nagged at the back of my head: 'This isn't right. Why should I not tell anybody where I'm going?' It was weird, if not crazy. But I didn't listen to my instincts. It was not like me; this was my gut instinct shouting at me – how much louder did it have to be before I'd listen? As I drove to Kenny's, I kept asking myself why a friend would ask me not to tell anybody where I was going. Nevertheless, I set out to go and rescue my buddy.

It took me more than half an hour to find his house – in a cul-de-sac. The lack of street lights didn't help much. I stopped outside his place and took a quick look around (an old habit I'd been taught in karate).

I slowly made my way towards the front door. The veranda lights were off and, as I couldn't see much, I listened closely for any noises coming from the inside of the house. Everything was quiet. I noticed that there was no car parked outside, but this seemed the only way in. Had the guys who had come to 'fuck up' Kenny entered the house somewhere else? I knocked on the door.

As I waited for Kenny to come to the door, the voices in my head screamed, 'Leave!' But still I didn't listen. Kenny directed me to the back of the house from behind the closed front door.

'I don't have the keys to unlock the door,' he said.

'How odd,' I thought.

I hobbled down the steps to the back garden, stumbling on my crutches, warning voices still talking in my head. I was scared, but I shuffled on. As I pushed open the back gate, Kenny was standing there. He seemed to be burning what looked like credit cards on the braai in the back yard – but I still didn't listen to my gut instinct.

'Did you see anybody when you came in the gate?' he mumbled. 'You must have seen them, they're standing right there.'

I realised at that moment that the man was delusional. Nobody was coming to beat him up.

'Do you have training in self-defence if confronted with a gun? Did they teach you that in martial arts?' Kenny asked.

I decided to dodge the question. 'Martial arts is not really about fighting. I prefer to walk away from confrontations,' I said.

But he insisted: 'Did they teach you how to defend yourself against a gun in martial arts?'

Now I was really scared. The target was *me*, and nobody knew where I was. A man on crutches with only one good leg is pretty defenceless.

I tried to keep him talking: 'Where are these guys?'

He didn't answer. I watched him closely. His eyes suddenly drew into slits and the next moment he was raising his arm and pointing at my face. I heard a deafening noise, saw a bright flash and then felt the impact of an object brushing past my face – a .38 Special.

He had hit me on the side of my head with the gun, at the same time pulling the trigger. At first I thought it was a toy. Who plays with real guns? But my eardrum was ringing and I smelt the acrid odour of gunpowder. Kenny had actually fired the gun! And as it was a real gun, it had to be a real bullet. My vision blurred; my mind raced.

'What are you doing?' I yelled, leaping away from him.

My mouth was dry and I was shaking like a leaf. I looked straight into his eyes. He was not there at all – his eyes were dead. He showed no emotion. It was all a game to him. Then Kenny aimed the gun at my forehead and fired another shot. I heard the bullet thud into the back door of the house. He had missed – God knows how when he was so close by!

I suddenly became very calm. It was as if I knew I was about to die, almost as if something else was taking over (as though the Divine had taken control of my life). I was in a nightmare, but this was Kenny's nightmare, not mine. I tried desperately to calm him down (hoping it would have some effect on me too!) by trying to reason with him.

At the same time, I was slowly edging backwards, scanning the surrounding space for a possible escape route. Weighing up my options, I made a dash for the back door, hoping to make it into the kitchen. I made it through, but with a wedge under the door, I couldn't slam it shut. The third shot slammed into the door, just inches from my face.

'Kenny, we need a cup of coffee,' I said, shaken to the core as he entered the room.

There was a deathly pause, and then he nodded. Mumbling incoherently, he indicated to me to sit down while he made it. In my head I kept repeating, 'Keep things together.' I had to be sharp now. Propped up against the kitchen wall was a 12-gauge shotgun. It was like an arsenal in there – he was ready for the 'enemy'. Sadly, the war was in his head.

Kenny proceeded to pour out his woes. His wife was filing for divorce and for custody of their children (I couldn't say I blamed her). 'People' were after him. The people in question were the police – although he had left the Force years before, he had witnessed acts of torture.

'Now they are coming for me,' he said. 'There are these guys in my head – I have dreams all the time.'

On and on he babbled, alternately slugging alcohol from the bottle and sipping coffee. Then he put the gun down on the table. 'Should I grab it and shoot him?' I wondered. I didn't think I had the ability to kill; the thought alone was enough to turn me to stone. Thoughts raced through my head: 'Will he read my mind and get to the gun before me? Will he realise that I wanted to kill him?'

I told myself to stop thinking these things. 'Concentrate,' I said to myself. 'Get out of here alive and in one piece.'

'Does anybody know where you are?' Kenny suddenly asked.

I lied: 'Janine does.'

'You need to go home to her.'

I nodded without any hesitation.

Then he asked, 'Can you possibly drop off some Christmas presents for my daughter?'

Again I nodded. All I wanted to do was get out of there alive. I would have agreed to almost anything. I stumbled calmly towards the door, my legs like jelly, my heart pounding. Would he change his mind at the last minute?

Then a fourth shot rang out, going just over my head. I didn't turn around – his laughter told me that the game was still on; he was still manic. As I clambered over the back gate (there was no time to fiddle with niceties), another bullet whizzed past my head. He was a proficient marksman, so the near misses were obviously deliberate.

I stumbled towards the road. Would he make it to the front

of the house before I could get into my car? I was parked the wrong way round in the cul-de-sac. Reverse? My mind didn't even go there. I turned the car around, but I still had to pass Kenny's house. But he didn't make an appearance. I revved the engine – anybody listening would have thought I was in a drag race – and drove off as fast as I could.

I didn't look back, just in case he'd suddenly appeared. I didn't want to see him ever again. I was doing what a child sometimes does – I closed my eyes: 'If I can't see you, then you can't see me.' I put the radio on – any distraction helped – but it just emitted a really odd sound. Strange, as it had been working perfectly well when I arrived. I fiddled a bit with the dial, twisting it back and forth. Then it dawned on me: it was my ears that were ringing. There was nothing wrong with the radio – the shots had temporarily deafened me.

I drove home in record time. I had to talk to someone, but nobody was there. I phoned my cousin Keith and told him the whole story. In my confused state of mind, I might have said that I had *been* shot rather than being shot *at*. With all the ringing in my ears I couldn't hear well, so I ended up going to his house while he came to mine. I sat outside his place, wondering where he had disappeared to.

Half an hour later Keith pitched up with his girlfriend, Michelle. Over cups of strong coffee, I repeated my story. I was in a quandary about what I should do. Michelle suggested we call the police and have Kenny arrested.

Keith said, 'Let's lure Kenny over and beat him up for all the anxiety he has caused you and *then* call the cops.'

Common sense told me that I should listen to Michelle, but

Keith could be persuasive. So Keith called Kenny to come and settle the issue. Kenny answered the phone right away.

'I'll come, but if Stephen's there, I'll finish him off!' he said.

Keith ordered me and Michelle into the back garden to wait. We were not happy; it was the middle of the night – or rather the early hours of the morning. Kenny arrived within minutes. After we'd spent an hour in the garden, I woke the neighbours to ask if I could use their phone. Half asleep, they agreed. We phoned Keith. He answered, reporting that he and Kenny were having a drink and listening to music.

Michelle and I went back into the garden. About an hour later, we heard a loud thud. Silence. Another thud. Then Keith was walking towards us, his hands and upper body covered in blood.

'Now you can call the police,' he said.

But the cops had no available vehicles to send round, so we would have to wait our turn. In the meantime Keith told us what happened. Apparently Kenny had tried to take a shot at him, but Keith had lunged for the gun and grabbed it, simultaneously smashing Kenny's head against the wall. Kenny had begun to laugh, making Keith realise he was definitely insane *and* as hard as nails. Any other person receiving a blow that severe would have been knocked unconscious. So Keith smashed Kenny's head against the wall again – this time knocking him out cold.

Kenny was still lights-out an hour and a half later when the police arrived and hauled him into the back of their van. We followed the van back to the station, where we laid a charge of attempted murder. Later that day, I started thinking that this idiot might actually get out of prison one day and come looking for me again. So I went back to the station and dropped the charges. I thought it was the best way to forget about the whole ugly incident.

I finally made my weary way home, where Janine was waiting. I told her all the gory details, and then she asked, 'Is Kenny okay?'

Kenny? Her question hit me in the pit of my stomach. Why did she show no concern for me? Did she not care how I was feeling – was she not even interested in knowing if I had any injuries? No – her only concern was for a man who had tried to kill her future husband!

It was a turning point in our relationship.

And my sister's response? Almost as bad. She kept asking, 'Why did he want to kill you? What did you do to him?' Now I really needed emotional support. My only mistake had been to try to help a friend in need, but now I had begun to feel guilty about going to 'help' Kenny, as the intensity of everyone's questions threw me. At least my parents, thank goodness, believed me, and they tried to persuade me to see a therapist. The 'tough boy' ignored their advice.

'Don't be silly, I'm fine,' I said.

But my fiancée siding with Kenny? Deep inside my heart, something died that night. I was still very much in love with Janine, but had my head been stronger than my heart, our relationship would have been history. Instead, I followed my heart: we bought a house together and began to talk about our future. Hope always springs eternal.

Then the issue of children came up. I thought we had crossed that bridge eighteen months before. But now Janine, a Catholic, said she wanted a child of her own and that artificial insemination was out of the question for her.

My job as a printer entailed shift work – but Janine was doing shifts of a different nature. At the time, the night shift was paying more money than the day shift, and we were working towards our future: a new house, marriage and all the pleasant aspects of life. We had some lengthy conversations about making our dreams come true sooner, and we agreed that in order to do so, I would work night shift for a trial period of six months.

The first couple of months went well, or so I thought. In the early days of our relationship, Janine was quite happy to stay at home and watch television or read when I was at work. Then one evening Janine said that she wasn't sure if she wanted this any more. She was lonely.

'What do you mean?' I asked.

She said that she was leaving for Cape Town in the morning; she needed time to think.

I tried to convince her to stay. Eventually I asked, 'Janine, how long have you been thinking about doing this?'

'A couple of weeks.'

'Why didn't you say anything before?'

'I wasn't sure how to,' was all she would say.

I begged her to stay. 'What have I done wrong?' I asked.

'Nothing! It's me,' was all she'd say.

She had made up her mind.

That night I lay wide awake, wondering what I had done to drive her away. I hoped she would change her mind. I finally fell asleep, and when I woke up, she was gone. No Janine.

The next couple of days passed in a haze. My friends told me not to worry.

'Things will come right,' they said. 'You will meet somebody who'll appreciate you.'

A month passed. Then, as I was about to start my shift one day, a colleague said there was a telephone call for me. I picked up the receiver and heard Janine's voice asking for forgiveness: a shock-punch to my stomach.

'I made a mistake! I want to come back to you,' she said.

My head urged me to tell her to piss off, but my heart was saying differently. Eventually I agreed to have her back.

'But we need to talk,' I said.

'Whatever you decide, I'll go along with it,' she said.

I made arrangements to meet her at a local restaurant the next evening. 'What are you doing? Are you mad?' I kept asking myself, but my heart was crying out for Janine. The next day I had mixed feelings; I wasn't certain what to do. But then, when we saw each other, all the anger I had felt vanished instantly. We just hugged and kissed – in those few seconds every problem we'd had disappeared, all the doubts just vanished. Later, Janine came home with me, where we made passionate love. All was well again with my world: Janine was back in my arms.

It was only a few days later that I knew that I had to have answers to my questions before we could move on.

'Janine, tell me why you came back,' I insisted.

'I really missed you and I realised I had made a mistake,' she said.

I asked her about Cape Town: 'Where did you stay?'

'With a friend in Pinelands.'

'Male or female?'

'Does it matter?'

'Yes,' I said.

'Female.'

I knew in the back of my mind that she was lying, but I decided that despite that, we should try to move on. And things did go well enough for a while, but one night when I finished work early and arrived home, Janine was nowhere to be found. I phoned her close work associate and asked if she was with her. Janine's colleague stuttered and stammered, saying Janine was on her way home, but I knew it wasn't true. On another night I phoned our house and a stranger answered the phone. At first I thought I might have the wrong number, as I didn't recognise the man's voice, but I knew that this wasn't so.

Our relationship finally ended when Janine said that she needed to be on her own. She moved out. I didn't hear much news of her – until a couple of months later, when I phoned her company for her forwarding address; by chance, her friend answered and told me that Janine was pregnant. I simply told her colleague to send Janine my regards, said goodbye and put the receiver down.

But in reality I felt as if I had been kicked in the stomach. I could feel the tears welling up, and then all the pent-up anger and frustration of all the rejections seemed to sweep over me all at once. I sat and wept non-stop for more than an hour. Afterwards I felt some relief – it had been a long time since I had let go in this way. In fact, a burden lifted because, in my heart, I had always suspected that Janine had not been faithful. It was all over now, and I finally had closure.

So this was life as an adult with Klinefelter's syndrome, I thought. I felt and looked normal, as far as I could tell – yet I still longed for love and acceptance. I was at an age where I wanted to settle down with a partner. All my peers were marrying and having kids, but this was not going to be part of my reality, which I just had to accept. Deep inside, I was convinced that there was someone out there for me and that I would just have to be patient. My perspective deepened: I came to see that life has a strange way of putting incidents or traumas in my path so that I can make the changes necessary to move on.

Shortly after Janine and I split up, I decided I'd had enough of standing behind a printing machine. I wanted to do something else instead of working the night shift. On those shifts, I got on well with a guy named Eddie, and we had some good laughs. But I wanted to do something else with my days.

One evening Eddie said to me, 'Have you ever thought about selling?'

'Selling what?'

'Any type of selling!'

'Why do you ask?'

'I've been watching you, and you are different from the rest of the guys here,' he said. 'I don't think you fit in here. You can do better for yourself.'

Eddie had planted a seed in my mind. I thought about his suggestion. I realised I didn't want to stand behind a machine all my life. I thought perhaps I could ask the floor manager to give me a chance to sell printing for the company. The next day I plucked up the courage to approach him.

But he looked at me as if I had slapped him in the face and said, 'You are not a salesperson. That's a special type of person.'

'Give me a chance,' I said. 'Just one month, and if I don't prove myself, you can kick me out. What do you say?'

He looked at me for a moment and said, 'Nah! I don't think so; you don't have the right personality.'

I was shocked by his answer, but I could see I was wasting my time.

I wasn't going to leave it there, though. In October 1989, I approached my brother, who had his own office automation company, and asked him to teach me how to sell. He brushed my request aside. So I pushed him – I wasn't going to give up. I asked him to give me a chance and, if I didn't make it in two or three months, he could tell me to leave. He said he would think about it.

A week later he called me to his offices in Germiston and said, 'I'll give you a try at the beginning of the year, but I'm not going to promise you anything. And if you stuff up, you're out.'

'Great,' I replied.

I went back to work and handed in my resignation. In the printing trade, you have to give only one week's notice. I gave them two months' notice, and told them I wanted to go back onto the day shift. When the floor manager heard of my resignation, he came storming down the stairs.

'So! You think you're going to make it out there?'

'Yes,' I said.

'You'll see! You'll come crawling back to us. Do you think you are better than us?'

I have always been amazed when people make that kind of statement. When you want to move on in your life, this somehow seems to affect people in odd ways.

Everybody suddenly gave me the cold shoulder, but Eddie said, 'Just ignore them. They're a bunch of wankers.'

I joined the five employees working at my brother's company in 1990. Johnny gave me a Dictaphone.

'Go home and talk into this and listen to your own voice,' he advised. 'Another thing: talk into the mirror.'

This exercise put me off a bit, but I was determined to go for it. Johnny put me with another guy who'd been in printing and I accompanied him initially. He had a very different way of selling – pretty rough at times – but people liked him well enough and would buy from him. I went out with other sales-people as well, learning a bit from each of them. Eventually I was given the job of cold-canvassing the Johannesburg City area – a very difficult way of selling.

I remember the first time I had to go out on my own. I stopped outside the building where I was going to canvass, gearing myself up for the trial ahead: getting out of the car, looking at the building. The idea was to start at the top floor and work my way down. Instead, I turned around and went home. The next day my brother asked me how it had gone.

'Fine,' I lied.

But I knew I had to conquer my fear, so I went back to the building and told myself, 'Do it. Move forward and don't think.'

In the first office, I stuttered to start with and soon felt the sweat pouring off me. It wasn't even a hot day, but it sure was hot in my head! Thank God the receptionist picked up on my inexperience and told me to take it slowly and relax. That day was one of the hardest days in my early selling career. After that, the rest was easy. I got better and better as my confidence grew.

Years later, when I had my own successful printing business, I bumped into that stupid, short-sighted manager from the printing company at which I'd once worked. He had heard that I had my own company.

'Come and sell for me,' he said.

'Why didn't you give me a chance before?' I asked, but I didn't even wait for the answer. I walked away, got into my car and drove off.

Six months after my break-up with Janine, I met a girl through Paul, a friend I had made on the night shift at the printing company. Paul's wife, Anne, had asked if I might be interested in meeting Karen, a lovely Englishwoman from her office. I said I would, but I waited a day or two before I called; I wasn't certain if I wanted to meet someone. But then I thought, 'Why not?'

Karen and I arranged to meet at a coffee shop – if we didn't like each other, we could part ways then and there. When I saw her, I realised I'd been expecting somebody with a much younger personality than me. I was surprised at how confidently she carried herself – she was only twenty. She had long, light-brown hair and was about five foot five. I thought she was very pretty – slim, with lovely green eyes.

The moment we introduced ourselves, we just clicked. We liked the same music and discovered we had similar values. We started to see more of each other and always had a great time, but there was one snag: she really wanted to have children with the right man. I knew that in the next couple of days I would have to tell her that I couldn't have children. I broke the news to her one afternoon over coffee. She said it would not matter; she could always adopt.

'Are you sure there won't come a time when you will want your own children?' I asked her.

But she said no, that would not happen.

We had been seeing each other for a couple of months

when Karen started talking about children and pushing for us to get married. I told her I had been engaged six months before and married two years before. I didn't want to rush into anything just yet.

I sat down one evening and thought things through, and I knew I had to end the relationship. Karen's feelings for me were stronger than mine were for her. I believed that she could do better with somebody else, with whom she could have children. I didn't want her to have any regrets. Karen was devastated when I broke up with her, convinced that it was her fault.

I assured her that she was a wonderful woman.

Shortly afterwards, she met somebody else. I would like to think that she found happiness.

I was alone again. I had always thought a marriage or a relationship would be complete if two people really loved each other. Yet, I had to be truthful: almost every woman (certainly, all the women I'd met) wanted children of her own. Adoption or artificial insemination was not an option. I was now thirty-one and wanted a lasting relationship. Every time I mentioned that I was sterile, the relationship changed irrevocably: we wouldn't meet as often, or the woman refused contact, or she just wanted 'to be friends'.

I finally understood that any future woman in my life would need to either have kids of her own already, or not want any. People assume that because I couldn't have children, I didn't desire them. I would dearly have loved a child of my own, but I was more adaptable, simply because I had to be. Living with Klinefelter's syndrome made me become a little more philosophical. I would simply have to wait for the right person to come along. I was lonely, but I was learning how to cope on my own.

After the break-up, I stayed on in the house Janine and I had bought together, which was a mistake; it brought bad luck. Burglars broke in three times in the space of six months and cleaned me out. At first, the insurance did pay out, but the burglars seemed to know when something had been replaced, and returned for it. The third time the insurance company didn't pay out – I must have been assessed as too much of a risk or been suspected of having had a hand in the burglary.

In that time I met a woman who was thirty-four and had a ten-year-old son, Donny. Susan was born in Hungary but had come to South Africa at the age of twelve. Finally I felt that I had met my match. It wouldn't matter that I was sterile – we could live happily ever after, as Susan had Donny. Susan suggested that I move in with her to get away from the bad memories left by the burglaries. When I did, a month later, it was literally with just the clothes on my back.

This was probably one of the most testing periods of my life. On the one hand, I had wanted somebody who had her own child and didn't want any more children. On the other, I wondered what it would be like to raise someone else's child.

I remember when Donny and I met. I was in Susan's lounge, finishing a cup of coffee and about to leave, when Susan said, 'Stick around for a while.' Her ex-husband was dropping Donny off and she wanted the boy to meet me. After five minutes, a key turned in the door and in walked Donny. He was small, like any other kid his age, with blond hair and blue eyes, unlike his mother – she had brown eyes. He sat down on the couch. I wasn't sure what to do, so I just said, 'Hello.'

He replied, 'Do you want to see my toys?'

That was the start of my relationship with Donny. Susan told me afterwards that he had never done that with anybody before. She had been quite shocked, but felt it was a great start. I treated Donny as if he were an adult, which worked well for us. I prefer the adult–adult rather than the adult–child way of relating. Over the next few months, I settled in nicely.

But then Donny started having problems at school. This brought about its own set of challenges and put pressure on my relationship with Susan.

She was struggling to discipline Donny on her own, and I suggested she allow me to get involved. At first she was reluctant. Then, when she was at the height of her frustration, trying to get him to do his homework, the school called her: Donny had not done any of his assignments for the past three months, they reported. They wanted to know what was going on. Susan turned to me for help.

That evening we sat down for a talk after dinner. We decided to limit Donny's television and computer time until he proved he could get his assignments done. Donny joined us and he glared at me when I told him of our decision. Then he stormed out of the room.

We waited. A couple of minutes later Donny came back in and said, 'Fine.'

The plan worked well for a couple of months, but then Donny started slipping back into his old routine. This time his mother threatened him with boarding school, saying she would give him until the end of the year to prove himself. But we couldn't watch him twenty-four hours a day, so he was soon back to his old tricks. The following year, when he would progress to

Standard 3, we decided that he should go to boarding school. I wasn't crazy about this decision – I am not particularly fond of boarding schools – but Susan viewed this as the best available option. She was proved right: Donny's marks soon improved and he seemed to enjoy school much more.

Sometimes my relationship with Donny took strain. I suppose we were both to blame for this. I was trying to be both his friend and his parent, and this didn't always work. He took advantage of it. We had some great times, but there were bad times too. Whereas Donny felt I disciplined him too harshly, I thought I was in the right. Looking back now, I probably was too strict with him. It's hard to bring up other people's children. Susan often took Donny's side, and I always told her not to do this in front of him. But I am glad I was with them at that time – I would like to think I made a positive impact on Donny's life.

My professional life was also undergoing a huge change. My decision to start my own company had its origins in my years of working for bosses – I often felt I worked harder than they did. One day, by chance, I glanced at a cost sheet and saw the amount of money the company was making. I was horrified that the employees were being paid such a pittance while the company was making so much profit. A seed was planted.

'I've always been able to motivate myself,' I thought, 'so running my own business can't be that hard.' I was also a reliable person, so I knew that would give me a head start. The best way to find out whether I could do it or not was to go out there and try it. And I did. I tried both selling and starting a small business of my own, beginning with stationery and other types of printing.

For five years, life couldn't have been better. I was running my own printing company and I was in a steady relationship. I felt secure with Susan, and I could concentrate on my business. My clients were satisfied with the company's service and referred us to friends and business associates.

My business grew and did exceptionally well. Donny, Susan and I were getting on much better. I was also earning more money and, for a change, Susan and I could afford to go on holidays. And Donny was thriving at school. But whenever I think things are just dandy, something bad happens. Is it Stephen's Law?

Of course Susan and I had our ups and downs, like most couples. Every so often a troubling aspect would creep into our relationship. Susan could be insecure, especially around other women. I always tried to reassure her that I was happy with her, but she'd just get irritated and call me a 'wimp'. When I was out on the road, she fretted about me and the women I might meet. I really wasn't interested in anyone else – I'm a one-woman man and I didn't want anything to harm our relationship. I did sometimes visit a mutual friend of ours, Louise, but only as a friend. She lived on my route and I'd stop at her place for a break. It was merely convenient; I just wanted a friendly chat.

I suppose I should have known that this would make Susan jealous. In the evening, I'd mention that I had popped in at Louise's. Susan didn't like it at all. I got grilled: Why did I have to visit Louise? Was I attracted to her? I assured Susan that I wasn't, but I'm sure at the back of her mind she thought differently. I see her insecurity now and realise I shouldn't have provoked it by visiting her friend, even for a social chat. At the time I thought that as long as I told Susan, she would be fine with it.

But I was generally content with Susan, my business was growing and Susan and I had decided to buy a house together. But something else was going on inside me. I felt an anger deep inside me that would come and go. I wondered why I wasn't man enough to make Susan feel secure and make us both happy.

A friend of Susan's, Eddie, told us his life had changed for the better since he'd been seeing a therapist. I thought a lot of the anger I felt was linked to the Kenny incident, which I had not resolved in my mind. But Susan was against therapy.

'You'll get over the incident in time,' she said. She was worried that I would change and that that would affect our relationship.

Nevertheless, I contacted a therapist, Gail, and for the next year I attended sessions. I talked and gradually unravelled. Gail believed I was suffering from trauma. We backtracked over the previous five years, as I was trying to get over the past. I had basically blocked Kenny from my memory and shut that night out. Gail diagnosed post-traumatic stress disorder and, when none of the therapy seemed to help me, she tried hypnotherapy.

One morning, I went into Gail's consulting room expecting a session like every other. But when I sat down, she started off by asking me to imagine that she was Kenny.

'What would you want to say to me?' she asked.

I looked at her as if she was mad, shook my head and said nothing. She repeated the question and told me to breathe deeply. I could feel the emotion rising and tried to stop it.

'Let it go,' she said softly.

I quietly started to cry and said that I would like to kill her (him).

I said, 'I am so upset at how you fucked up my life.'

Then it all came out. I actually started to visualise that Gail was Kenny, which she sensed. She started talking quietly again, telling me to breathe deeply and to relax.

Finally we got to the crux of the matter – that I had felt betrayed and abandoned by the people closest to me. There was my father and his unpredictable moods; my brother Johnny and his bullying; the teasing at school; the struggles of growing up; the betrayal of the doctor and my mother, who had failed to protect me from him. All of this had been festering away inside of me. Then, finally, as if it were the last straw, there was the Kenny incident: the people I'd turned to – my sister and Janine – had not been there for me.

I cried so much, I thought my body would run out of water.

I could now sympathise somewhat with men returning home after experiencing the horrors of war. One can only imagine what they must have been through and how they may struggle to explain it to others, who will never really understand. Even if people experience the same incident, each one's trauma is unique, and the scars left are different too.

Susan and I were still living together, but the relationship had changed (as she had predicted). In my mind I believed she had betrayed me too, even though she wasn't even there on the night in question (or during my childhood). I believed I had lost a part of me that night at Kenny's and it had not yet been retrieved, not even in the therapist's rooms.

My sessions with Gail continued, as did the emotional churning up discussing the past. Eventually Susan withdrew her support from me as I went on with the therapy. She was constantly expecting me to come home after a session and drop some bombshell on her. Her insecurities were simply too big for the both of us. She had wanted to help me by allowing my visits to Gail, but then she couldn't cope with her fears that I might change. And I *had* changed – when I came home after an hour's session of emotional turmoil, I wanted to be able to talk to somebody at home, but Susan couldn't handle that. I was emotionally vulnerable and wanted to run far, far away from life – or just myself.

Perhaps I had changed at a deep level, and it was that that was affecting our relationship. The sessions with Gail had unearthed memories and emotions that were difficult to deal with. I honestly didn't know whether or not I still wanted to be with Susan. My feelings had changed; Susan's insecurities troubled me. Although she said she wanted to help me, she was more concerned with whether our relationship would survive than with giving me support.

I continued to practise martial arts. I loved t'ai chi, which allowed my mind to slow down so that I could enter a different space. Some people think t'ai chi is only for sissies. But in my experience, the martial arts – karate, ju-jitsu and the like – help you develop character. Only our own ignorance makes us judge others. In t'ai chi, I found a martial-art form that suited me perfectly. Its movements were much slower than any form I had previously tried, taking me into a deeper place.

Sometimes, just holding the move keeps one's mind in the moment. Even the breathing is different; one takes much deeper breaths. I wondered how it was possible for anybody to get fit practising t'ai chi – it seemed so passive. Yet I would often collapse into bed when I got home from a practice session, to sleep soundly until morning. T'ai chi certainly helped me survive the stressful times with Susan.

And also strengthened me for what lay ahead ...

21

Living among robbers

Growing up in South Africa in the 1970s was hard. It was a society led by dominant males – our teachers, fathers, army leaders and government figures were tough, aggressive men. There was little place for softies like me. Now, in the new South Africa, born in 1994, I wondered about my role. The new government had promised democracy and freedom for all, but they were failing to control the violent crime that threatened to destabilise their initiative. Johannesburg reminded one of the Wild West, with people running around carrying illegal guns. But it wasn't quite like the old Westerns Luis and I had once watched: the rules had changed. I so wanted to be part of the new South Africa, the buoyant excitement of it, but I found the reports of violent crime frightening.

One morning, I'd arranged to meet Susan and a client, who wanted a new design for his company logo, at Grayston Drive Mall in Sandton. Susan was a graphics whizz – a great help in my printing business. As I was driving into the parking lot, I passed a green security van. Ahead, I saw four men wielding AK-47s.

Everything around me slowed down. The men were holding up the van, regardless of the fact that I was right there, witnessing the robbery. All of a sudden they started shooting at the guards over and around my car. By some miracle, not one bullet hit my car. Then the cops arrived, followed shortly by a police helicopter hovering above the scene.

I couldn't really believe what I was seeing. One minute I was looking for a parking bay and was about to pull into it, and then the next a man appeared in front of my car, walking slowly and steadily towards the four men with the machine guns. I saw him raise his arm; in his hand was a gun. He calmly fired a shot over my car at one of the gunmen. The hijacker fell down – just like in the movies – the only difference being that he didn't stand up again. And half of the side of his head was missing. I drove into the parking bay and just sat frozen for a moment. Had I dreamt the past few minutes?

A plain-clothes policeman asked, 'You okay?'

I sat there feeling completely numb, shell-shocked, staring at him. Susan arrived ten minutes later. I told her what had happened, regained a little composure, and we went off to see the client.

But I was severely shaken up. Afterwards I felt jittery and anxious and I couldn't sleep – the drama kept replaying itself in my mind. If this or that had happened, if I had reacted or got out of the car ... Then I buried the trauma deep inside, as was my wont.

Eventually, life settled down again. Susan and I both had jobs and a nice home – we even had two dogs and three cats. Everything was going rather well.

One day Frankie, our female chow, was out of sorts. She had recently been spayed, and although she was not on heat, she was still giving off a scent. Neighbourhood dogs scaled the walls regularly to get to her. On the advice of friends, we tried putting citronella oil along the wall. This kept the dogs off our property for a while, but they soon got used to the smell. Another friend then suggested razor wire. I went out and bought a couple of strips, parked back at home and went into the house to get a tape measure. I couldn't have been more than a couple of minutes. Back at the wall, I reached up to take a measurement and suddenly noticed that my neighbour had a car just like mine – same colour, make and registration.

What was I thinking? It *was* my car!

But why were there four people in my car and why was it parked outside my neighbour's house?' It took me a couple of seconds to catch on. Then I jumped over the wall and ran down the road, shouting at the arseholes to get out of my car. My cellphone was bouncing around in my pocket, so I took it out, grasping it in my hand. I raised my hand in the air, screaming like a madman.

On hearing me, the men jumped from the vehicle – two disappeared in opposite directions, the other two were coming towards me. I lashed out and hit the man closest to me. His step faltered – he stumbled, righted himself and ran off. The second man had a gun in his hand. Before he could take aim, I hit him hard on the side of the head with the cellphone (the early models were nice and chunky).

He kept shouting, 'Don't shoot!'

He must have thought my cellphone was a gun. The two of us struggled until my phone broke in two. In the process, the man dropped his gun. As I grabbed him by the shirt, he howled in agony.

'Why is he screaming?' I wondered, as he broke free and ran off. My hand still clutched part of his shirt – and in it a chunk of flesh.

I chased after the men for about a hundred metres, until a passer-by shouted, 'They've got guns!' Then I decided to make my way back to the car. I was lucky to be alive – again I'd survived a near catastrophe. I took stock of the situation, assessing the damage to the car. The steering column would need fixing. The repairs would eventually cost R10 000, but at least I still had my car.

It's said that bad things always happen in threes. One night, a few months after the car-theft attempt, I was about to leave for a t'ai chi class, when I felt a little uneasy. I didn't know what was causing the feeling, so I locked the dogs in the house – something I never usually did.

We had bought the house not long beforehand, and had not yet fitted automatic gates. I reversed down the driveway to the roll-up gate, which was bordered by high walls – a security measure typical of Johannesburg. Once outside the gate, I jumped out of the car and rolled the gate back down. Suddenly I heard a noise from behind the car, and my heart immediately started beating faster. Two guys were striding towards me. One, who was carrying a gun, shouted, 'Get into the car and drive!' and then, 'Check if he's got a gun!'

His accomplice of about sixteen frisked me. I took a chance and threw the keys to the other thug, who looked about eighteen, saying, 'Here, take the car.' Then I walked around to the driver's side and came face to face with him. He was just a kid. I am sure that I would have seen the gun shaking in his hand had I not been so nervous myself.

'Turn off the immobiliser! Start the car!' he yelled at me.

The younger guy shouted, 'Kill him! Kill him!'

The older one promptly smacked me on the top of my head with the gun. I looked straight into his eyes and said, 'Shoot me.'

He yelled at me to turn around.

I said, 'Look me in the eye and shoot. Look me in the eye, you little fucker, and then pull the trigger!'

But instead of killing me, he continued with the pistol-whipping. I wanted the ordeal to be over and I didn't care if it meant the end of my life. A second later, I realised that I could take him out, as his concentration and confidence were waning. But I held back – I was shaking like an old man.

'The best thing to do is to start the car,' I calculated. The keys were now in the ignition. I never thought I would think the sound of a car engine to be wonderful, but when I turned the key in the ignition that night, it was music to my ears. I stepped aside for the gunman, who climbed into the car with a smirk on his face: mission accomplished.

Or so he thought. He wound down the window, revving the engine, put the car into reverse, and pointed the gun at my stomach. Now that he had the protection of the car, he was full of bravado.

'Goodbye,' he said.

Time to run, but my legs had turned to stone. A cold sweat poured off my body. I only had seconds. Then something clicked in my head, and I started running. When I noticed a tree, I headed straight towards it. Then I heard the car cut out. As I was running, my mind was running alongside me, and it talked to me: 'Have you been shot? Or was that the exhaust backfiring?' The tree still seemed a million miles away. I finally reached it and slumped behind it, peering round the trunk to see where my assailants were. They had forgotten all about me and were driving off down the road.

I walked back home and seemed to wait for hours for Susan to answer the gate bell.

'Who's there?' she asked.

A faint whisper escaped my mouth.

She repeated the question, and I managed in a slightly louder voice, 'It's me.'

'Why aren't you using your keys?'

'I've been hijacked.'

Did she think I was fooling around – playing tok-tokkie, as if I were still a child? Stephen – the eternal child – teasing and playing silly buggers?

The news reported nine other hijackings that evening. I had had enough of living with the violence, and I had had enough of Johannesburg.

22

Bones, stones and endings

The warnings were too strong to ignore. Susan and I sold our house and, within a month, I'd sold my printing business too. We had decided to move south, to Cape Town.

My life with Klinefelter's syndrome seemed pretty normal by South African standards. Lack of testosterone had nothing to do with the events of late. Getting caught up in heists and being hijacked were just run-of-the mill events in the new South Africa. But I had suffered enough traumas and felt that I was attracting all the drama. 'Am I trying to prove my macho maleness after all?' I wondered. I wanted a safer, quieter life.

We liked Cape Town – it was a new start. We purchased a house in a quiet suburb about twenty kilometres from the centre of the city. Unfortunately we had forgotten our last move and the rigmarole it had involved; we might not have been so cavalier if we'd remembered. Crises have a way of kicking butt. The gods hand us these challenges and we usually view them in a negative light, but I believe all negatives can be turned to our benefit. Although I would never want to repeat going through a hijacking, a part of me thanks those guys. It turned my life around.

We made a new home and Susan and I found jobs relatively quickly. We settled into a routine again. Susan and I got on all right; we were both so busy making a new life that we probably didn't notice how pedestrian things had become between us. I liked the security of the relationship, even though there wasn't much passion. It all felt pretty normal to me, but I have no idea how Susan felt about it.

Once we were somewhat established in Cape Town, it was time for me to find a doctor for a routine check-up. I eventually booked an appointment with a local GP. Whenever I see a new doctor, I always disclose that I have Klinefelter's syndrome. This doctor advised me to make an appointment with a bone-disease specialist, who was based at the Provincial Hospital.

'A bone-density scan wouldn't go amiss,' she said.

I thought this rather odd. I was a man in his forties, not an eighty-year-old, but I thought it best to indulge her.

I was the youngest person in the waiting room by at least twenty years, and the others were mostly women. I felt uncomfortable – nothing new there. In time I was X-rayed – as I lay on the bed, the machine scanned my entire body, taking every bone into account. Then I waited for the results to be processed.

The doctor called me into his consulting rooms, a worried look on his face, and asked permission for a colleague of his to be present. No problem – I was used to being scrutinised. Then he dropped the bomb, which left me with the same feeling as when I was told, just before I was to be married, that I couldn't have children.

'You have osteoporosis. You have the bone density of a seventy-year-old man. You urgently need to take calcium to build up the bone.'

We all need a certain amount of calcium in our bodies, which builds up bone density and prevents us from getting osteoporosis. In men, calcium production is stimulated by testosterone. Men with Klinefelter's syndrome, however, do not produce enough testosterone, resulting in a calcium deficiency. The doctors had initially given me testosterone for only two years so that my body would be that of a normal eighteen-year-old's. Then they'd stopped the treatment. Over the years, without my realising it, my bones had just wasted away, up to the point where I had developed the early signs of osteoporosis. I suppose the doctors back then didn't have sufficient knowledge to know that treatment should be continued. Now, twenty years later, doctors know a lot more.

Although I should have continued the monthly injection of testosterone all along, testosterone has side effects, as I knew only too well – mood swings, heightened aggression, and an increase in confidence and libido. The doctor suggested that I go home and discuss the implications of resuming testosterone treatment with my partner, 'as the change may have varying effects on your relationship'.

I asked Susan to meet me for coffee so that I could tell her what had transpired: 'They recommend that we go for counselling.'

She brushed the advice aside: 'Come on – they're probably exaggerating.'

'No,' I said. 'I think they are quite serious about this.'

But Susan felt threatened. She must have thought I was using the impending treatment to get her to go for counselling.

'Are you telling me that they know how our relationship is?' she asked me accusingly.

'It's got nothing to do with that,' I assured her. 'They just think we both need to know what the issues are. These people know what they're talking about.'

But the suggestion had pressed Susan's buttons.

'How can a little bit of liquid change one so drastically? I think it's bullshit,' she declared.

I tried to argue: 'I'm sure that they've done tests before and have seen the results with other couples.' But it was useless.

'Do you *have* to have this?'

'Testosterone?' I asked. 'Yes, I have to. Without it, my bones will continue to crumble.'

The following week I began the new course of injections. No change occurred in the first few months; then, suddenly, it was as if somebody had turned on a light. I felt a new level of confidence – a bit like those early days when, at sixteen, I'd experienced the first changes because of the testosterone. I felt I could take on the world and more. However, there were some changes that neither Susan nor I enjoyed. I became increasingly aggressive – I was definitely getting in touch with my masculine side; it was the testosterone talking.

Small things began to bother me – for example, the gardening Donny and I did on Saturday mornings. I gardened with passion; he did it with a bit of resentment because we had told him to pull his weight. I always finished first and then called Donny to sweep up. Sometimes I had to call him more than once. Now that I was having the testosterone on a monthly basis, my fuse was suddenly shorter. I was becoming increasingly impatient with him because he didn't get going fast enough. This would not have bothered me before. I was also getting frustrated with Susan for the smallest of things.

The only good thing about the testosterone was that I had a lot more energy, which paid off when I cycled. Exercising now was great – less effort *and* less pain.

But I had a choice to make: either my bones fell to pieces or I had a personality change. I felt like a puppet whose strings were being manipulated. Susan and I started arguing more frequently, mostly over silly things. In comparison, before testosterone – the big T – I must have been a joy to live with. I had been a placid and sensitive man compared to the new Jekyll-and-Hyde me.

A further effect of the testosterone was that my libido increased tenfold. Instead of wanting sex twice a month, my desire increased to wanting to make love five times a week. There was more. Every twenty-one to twenty-five days, my emotions would ebb as the testosterone wore off. I would become tearful, my libido would die and my breasts would become tender and sensitive. I have a lot of sympathy for women: I understand all about sore breasts and how women suffer during their menstrual cycle.

Then there were the arguments with Donny. He was now sixteen and in the midst of adolescence. Only, I felt like an adolescent myself. Susan must have felt she had two teenagers to contend with. She should have listened to the doctors when they recommended counselling, as they obviously knew something we didn't.

Besides the monthly injection, I was supposed to supplement my calcium intake. On a pharmacist's recommendation, I started taking an over-the-counter product with approximately 1000 milligrams of calcium per dose. More side effects – this time kidney stones.

Kidney stones had to be the lesser of two evils, but a year later, my bone-density scan showed an increase of only one per cent.

'Surely that can't be right?' I thought.

It was time to do my own research. I surfed the Web, but

found little information on the disease or the medication with which to treat it. I was on the verge of giving up when a friend told me about a book called *Dead Doctors Don't Lie* – an immediate purchase.

The writer, Dr Wallach, became my overnight hero. According to him, kidney stones are caused when the body cannot absorb calcium. But an element called boron helps calcium bond to the bones. Wasn't this supposed to be fairly common knowledge to the average pharmacist? Sometimes I think that chemists and doctors merely help the pharmaceutical industry to get rich.

After much searching, I found some medication that contained boron, calcium and magnesium. The rest is history. I never went back for another bone-density scan. In a cycling accident a few years later, I should have had broken bones but walked away with only bruises.

In the midst of my medical trials, one evening in October 1996, my father collapsed and was rushed to Johannesburg General Hospital. The doctors were unable to diagnose any particular ailment, ascribing his condition to a bad fall at an advanced age – he was in his eighties.

Although I had moved to Cape Town, my parents and I were still close and I phoned them regularly. My father's moods had calmed down as he had aged; he just seemed a rather pathetic shadow of his former self.

After he had spent five days in hospital, the doctors operated on him without any explanation of the reason. He died under anaesthetic. I was traumatised. I hadn't even had the opportunity see him before his death. One always hopes that one will be able say goodbye to one's loved ones. Sometimes it is not to be.

About a week after my dad passed away, I received a call from the South African Police, who asked me whether I wanted to open a murder docket.

I asked why. The inspector told me that they suspected there had been negligence involved in my dad's death, and that it is standard procedure to open an investigation when someone dies on the operating table. He also said that one of the doctor's colleagues had called the police, as he had felt certain procedures had not been followed. The inspector didn't want to go into detail on the phone.

My father had already been an old man, and I could do very little, being so far away. The police investigation did not continue.

Shortly after my father passed on, Christine and I discussed what was best for our mother now that she was on her own. We decided to persuade her to move to Cape Town. We both felt that Mom's quality of life would be improved by living in the Mother City. Christine was busy; she had four children and was also studying to be a psychologist. So Susan and I found my mom a two-bedroomed house close to us, and she made the move. Mom's house had a garden and, once she started making acquaintances, she settled in quite happily.

In later years, she said, 'I wish I'd raised my kids here. It's so much better for family life.'

One day we went to Hout Bay to visit some friends of Susan's for lunch. They told us about Decorex, a very big exhibition that showcases decor, which they'd attended in Johannesburg. We discussed the possibility of Susan and I starting something similar, as there was nothing like it in Cape Town. As we were driving home, Susan and I started talking about the idea of putting together a show. When I had had my own printing company, I had specialised in printing for the exhibition and electronics industries. Susan's background was in the sales side of electronics.

Our friends, Jack and Brenda, who were involved in this kind of business, suddenly sprang to mind. They ran two exhibitions in Johannesburg. We contacted them, and after some negotiations, they offered us a partnership in a new business venture: they would hold 51 per cent of the shares to our 49 per cent. We would start our own interior exhibition business in Cape Town, which we would call Index. Susan and I would have to market the show, but they would finance it.

We decided to grab the opportunity, signed on the dotted line and had ourselves a deal. We were going into an industry in which neither of us had any experience, but we assured ourselves that we would be fine. The contract stipulated that we had six months to sell 50 per cent of the show. If we failed, we would have to pull the plug. Our new partners came to Cape Town for the launch at Bertie's Landing, a Waterfront restaurant, to which we invited all the media. And so Index was born in Cape Town.

In the 1990s, there were no major venues that could host conventions and exhibitions – the Cape Town International Convention Centre only came later. There were two viable options, though: the Good Hope Centre and the Culemborg Centre. We chose the latter for our first exhibition. Culemborg was a former central goods yard and storage plant, but had more recently been transformed into an exhibition centre. It was in a perfect location with loads of parking.

The business entailed selling exhibition space and then putting together the whole show. We also provided the internal structures for the exhibitions. We'd begin by sourcing clients who wanted to exhibit at the show and we'd sell stands of various sizes. These stands – white plastic panels supported by aluminium poles – came complete with plug points, fascia names and carpets.

We were successful almost immediately. Cape Town was fast becoming a local and international convention destination. Susan and I got stuck in and, six months later, we were eighty per cent full. Our first show was absolutely fantastic. Our space was completely sold out.

We ran the business successfully for three years. Then, a complete surprise: our partners wanted out and wished to sell their shares. The show had become our baby and had made an international mark, so they found buyers quickly and told us that a deal had been struck for us too. Our attorneys perused the contract. Thirty thousand rand later, paid out of our own pockets, their recommendation was not to accept the deal.

At first glance, it had all looked solid – with the offer of a R500 000 payout on condition that we both worked for the new company for a two-year period. It was a large company, which had absorbed many smaller companies under its name. But there was a lot of fine print in the contract, and the attorneys said that we would certainly lose out in the long term. However, if we refused the deal, we would probably walk away with only R100 000.

In the end, we decided not to accept the offer and lost our hard-earned cash. Were we disappointed? Yes; but the most disappointing aspect was losing respect for Jack and Brenda, two people we had thought were our friends. They had got what they wanted. Greed is not an endearing quality in anyone. Out of pocket, we had to start our lives over again.

Shortly after this, Susan and I started to argue much more often, mostly because of our lack of money – we were now both unemployed.

And there was another challenge. In the course of 1999, I began to study shiatsu, a Japanese pressure-point massage technique that focuses on clearing the blockages in the twelve 'meridians' of the body – a similar practice to acupuncture in traditional Chinese medicine. I was a natural at massage and healing. My 'patients' liked me and felt at ease with me. I did well in both the theory and the practical courses and passed all the exams. It seemed that my learning problems were finally a thing of the past – I had found a way of achieving.

After qualifying, I opened my own practice – an action that brought its own problems. Susan's insecurity surfaced again. She was not happy about me working with female clients. Shiatsu is a full-body treatment, although the patient remains fully clothed.

I believe a client–therapist relationship should remain professional. I am sure lines are crossed at times, but not if a therapist wants to make a success of his or her business, and I most certainly wanted to succeed. Shiatsu is a therapy that has great benefits for people, but Susan's constant fear was that I would fall for one of my clients. I tried to placate her, but the battle raged on, and her insecurity grew. This, coupled with the fact that she was not working and had too much spare time on her hands, signalled the end of our relationship in 2000. The nine-and-a-half-year contract was over.

At the ripe old age of forty-two, I moved into my mother's place. I felt as though I was going back to my childhood – instead of having a three-bedroomed house with my own possessions, I was now living in a single room surrounded by my mother's possessions. I found it hard to adjust – it was a difficult time. I had to tell my mother if I would be home for supper and, if I went out in the evening, let her know when I'd be home.

In addition, I had had to leave my 'children' with Susan. She had Donny, of course, but my animals – my dog Frankie and my cats Oscar, China and Nina – were like *my* children. I had poured my energies into caring for them. It took me many years to get over the loss of Frankie. Susan was angry and vengeful and wouldn't let me see the pets.

One of my fondest memories of Frankie was her joy when she was given biscuit treats. She would take a biscuit from her bowl and carry it around like a hot potato, tossing it in the air and trying to catch it in her mouth without letting it slip down her throat. Sometimes she flicked it into the air with her paw, as though playing with a mouse. If it fell on the floor, she would size it up for a while and then pounce. She would repeat this several times until the biscuit fell askew – and disappeared down her throat, unchewed. She always looked sad when this game came to an end.

After the break-up with Susan, I began to reflect on my relationships with women. The failures ate me up inside. I thought of Marina and the time I'd had to take the sperm-count test. 'Was this the underlying problem?' I wondered, as the test had reminded me of the sexual abuse I'd suffered. I realised that I had never really faced what had happened to me on the endocrinologist's examination table. Gail, the therapist in Johannesburg, and I had concentrated on the trauma caused by the Kenny episode, and not on the abuse. I had remained a victim of the abuse, and perhaps also of the bullying I had suffered at school. Although I had not yet considered therapy to deal with that trauma, I felt I needed to talk to someone. I could never have guessed that my healing would begin with my mom.

One evening we were watching a weekly magazine series on television together. The programme dealt with child abuse. I was eating the supper Mom had made, not really thinking about much while watching the story of a teenager's sexual abuse unfold on the TV screen. Then, suddenly, it felt as if the programme was directed at me. A wave of panic rushed over me and I felt like throwing up. All the memories came hurtling back. I suddenly felt ashamed to be with my mother. I got up quickly, almost knocking over the tray I was holding.

'What's the matter?' my mother asked.

I rushed to my room, so angry I felt like kicking down the door. Eventually I calmed down – I forced myself to keep it together. I knew my problem wasn't Marina or Susan's fault; it wasn't my mother's fault either. Then I began to cry, not fully understanding why. Perhaps I was crying for the child I'd seen on TV, perhaps for a failed relationship. The anger had come first, followed by huge sadness.

Finally the sobbing subsided and I returned to the lounge. My mom and I made tea and we sat down. Then I told her what had happened each time she took me to see the endocrinologist.

I was already in my mid-forties when I finally told my mother about what had happened behind the closed door of the specialist's consulting room. Up to that point, I had struggled through my relationships, fraught with insecurities. I told my mother of the experience with Marina and the sperm-count test, of how I'd suppressed any recollection of being sexually abused until that time. Then, it had felt as if I was reliving the experience. Only at that moment had I understood that I had been sexually abused as a young man.

My mother was extremely distressed that she had never acted on what she'd thought at the time was odd behaviour, and that she had never queried the frequency of the visits, thus saving me from the trauma I'd suffered. She tried hard to get me to share my pain, but my feelings were buried deep within me. I could, however, see how the experience had affected me and my sense of who I was. I looked for the positive in the situation too, though. The one positive that came out of the whole traumatic experience was the discovery that I had Klinefelter's syndrome and that I would, at least, get some relief thanks to the medication. But I still had many lessons to learn before I could heal completely.

After Susan and I separated, we had to stay in contact for the next few months so that we could dispose of the house. It didn't make the break any easier. After each time we met, I wondered whether I had made a terrible mistake – was it her I was missing, or just the animals?

I got up every morning at 4 a.m. to go cycling. Besides building muscle, the riding also gave me time to think. One morning, when I had been on the road for about half an hour, an inner voice told me, 'You've made a mistake. Phone Susan as soon as possible and tell her.' Whereas before I had been feeling quite happy, I now felt fraught. Should I call her, or should I just let things be?

I was following my usual route, over a hill. The next thing I knew I was flying over my bike's handlebars and crashing down onto my shoulder. A crunching sound as I hit the deck was instantly followed by pain. I had broken something.

My ju-jitsu training had taught me how to fall, so I had tucked my head in as I came down. Although it had saved my skull, it hadn't helped the shoulder. I lay there, trying to catch my breath and absorb the fact that I had crashed. Confused, I wondered what had gone wrong. My bicycle lay in the field beyond. Then I noticed some wooden planks lying in the road. I must have hit those. I hadn't even seen them in the dark – I was obviously doing too much thinking.

On reflection, I realise that I am always being tripped up when I'm about to do something I'm not meant to do. Sometimes I choose not to pay attention to the signs, but I am always warned. I credit my intuition for this – I wonder if it is more developed because of my extra x?

I managed to find my cellphone and dialled the emergency number. I was relieved when a voice answered on the other side.

'Where are you?'

I had no idea. The operator had picked up the call in Johannesburg and I was somewhere in the winelands of Durbanville.

'I'll dispatch an ambulance. Keep your phone connected. We can trace your whereabouts from the signal,' the operator instructed.

After what seemed like hours, the ambulance arrived and took me to Milnerton Medi-Clinic, where doctors treated me. I had a broken collarbone. The bike had come off better than I had – only its handlebars were slightly bent.

Now the warning – the one that I chose not to listen to (or perhaps hadn't understood) – came back to confront me. I needed a lift home from the hospital, but my mother didn't like driving far from home. So I phoned Susan, thinking she would happily help me out. I could also use the opportunity to tell her how wrong I had been to leave and, hopefully, could return home to her. But Susan's immediate response, without a moment's hesitation, was 'Catch a bus' before hanging up. Humans are strange creatures. Susan had previously declared her love for me and had told me what a wonderful person I was at the time of the break-up. She was not the one who wanted the relationship to end.

Some time later I discovered that my sister had made contact with Susan. I could only assume that she was trying to find out if the relationship could be mended. Christine, who had little contact with my girlfriends when we were dating, had a habit of making contact with them once the relationship was over. Was this where her professional role as a psychologist came in, wanting to help the wounded? I love my sister dearly, but I do not always understand her actions. Once again I had to give her the benefit of the doubt; maybe she had only been trying to help me.

In the meantime, my body slowly started to heal. A sling and rest were the only medicine I needed.

The shiatsu practice was ready to expand, and so I decided to go into business with two friends. We hired premises at the Blue Shed in the Victoria & Alfred Waterfront. A particular area had been designated for holistic health and was frequented mainly by tourists. I set up a stand and began offering massages. Soon I was busy enough and beginning to build up a steady clientele of both regulars and passers-by.

Then, in February 2001, I met Catherine. I was at the Blue Shed on a hot summer's day, working, when she arrived for a treatment. She was on holiday from Scotland. The connection was instant. We discovered that both our fathers had suffered from mood swings – her father had been schizophrenic. There was another coincidence – he, too, had descended from the French Huguenots.

I asked Catherine for her number, and we later met for coffee. We made small-talk and had a good time, going for dinner afterwards.

During Catherine's two-week stay in Cape Town, our relationship deepened. Once she had returned to Scotland, we wrote letters – good old snail mail – and often talked on the phone. After two months, we agreed that the time had come for me to go over to Scotland for a visit. I had not travelled abroad since my honeymoon with Marina in the early 1980s.

I arrived in Scotland at the end of May, with the countryside lush and green. I thought that it was the most beautiful country I had ever seen – besides South Africa – and I would learn that the people were friendly.

Catherine fetched me from the airport. As we drove down an old cobbled road, a wave of nostalgia washed over me: I had been here before. Everything was familiar. Was it a case of déjà vu? I knew I wanted to spend the rest of my life in Catherine's country. But after eight weeks and some wonderful times together, my money ran out. The exchange rate from rands to pounds was cruel, and though I did try to find a job, it was not to be.

And the relationship had begun to show cracks. I had noticed them before, but when one is in love, everything is rosy and one chooses to ignore the signs. Catherine suffered from bouts of depression and, as my departure day approached, she became increasingly distant. I suppose it was her way of coping with my imminent departure. I flew home to South Africa after a rushed goodbye, numb and hurt. Although, in my heart, I knew that our relationship was over, we continued communicating until December 2001. By then, our relationship had completely dissolved.

23

Passport control

After spending eight weeks in Scotland, I needed to get my working life back on track. I contacted my shiatsu clients, most of whom had said they would come back to me for treatment when I returned from Scotland. But my Scottish stay had run on longer than the planned three weeks, and many of my clients had found other therapists. For me, it was another wake-up call. I needed to put food on the table. After struggling for months, a client offered me a job selling advertising. I tried my hand at it, but it didn't work for me.

A few of my regular shiatsu clients remained loyal. One, Jimmy, I saw every Monday morning at his home, where occasionally I also worked on Nolene, a friend of his. I asked Nolene about herself – her health history and personal life – but she was a closed book. Most clients, I find, are a bit reserved to start with, but, as they relax, they start talking. Some of the information is important for the therapist to know.

Nolene, however, never got to the comfortable stage. She felt she was under interrogation. I had enough experience to rely on my gut instinct when treating her. Too bad I didn't listen to my gut when it told me to leave her be. But she intrigued me. I asked Jimmy to arrange a social meeting with her. I don't know why, as I had some reservations about her, but I didn't take heed. Jimmy, too, seemed reluctant (another warning bell?), but I persisted. Eventually we both attended one of Jimmy's parties.

Nolene, who was from England, had been in South Africa for two years and was trying to obtain her residency. Her parents were Irish, but she, her brother and her three sisters had grown up in Birmingham. This was all she would divulge. Maybe she thought I was an undercover immigration officer! I found her fascinating. The little voice in my head was urging caution, but Stephen wouldn't listen.

I asked Nolene out, in spite of my misgivings. She turned the date around and instead invited me for a meal at her place. We had a great evening, chatting about our daily lives, and how living in South Africa differed from living in the UK. I thought I was getting to know her ever so slightly. Driving home later, I reflected on the evening. Why was I not feeling more excited? A date usually puts me on a high – I get butterflies. But now all I had in my stomach was a burning sensation – either she was a bad cook or I was terribly nervous. There was also that little voice urging me to move on.

We saw each other for the next two weeks and, during one of our evenings together, the issue of my bicycle came up. My mother was constantly complaining about it having to be moved every time she wanted to use her car. Nolene seemed to have plenty of space in her garage.

'Could I perhaps leave my bike here until the tenants in my flat leave in November?' I asked her.

Anybody would have thought that I wanted to move in lock, stock and barrel. The evening suddenly came to an abrupt end – as did the pain in my stomach. Nolene didn't want me around; I was free to go.

But I can be stubborn. I ignored the nagging of my inner voice and tried to call Nolene. She wouldn't speak to me for two weeks – her phone was always on voicemail.

I wondered why she had reacted so strongly. I had to satisfy my curiosity. Our mutual friend – the go-between – Jimmy, cautioned, 'Be patient.' Eventually Nolene phoned me and we got back together again.

For a while, we sailed along on an even keel. Although the uneasy feeling in my stomach never abated, I believed I was in love. One evening, I asked Nolene to be my wife. As the words escaped my mouth, she accepted. We decided to marry in October 2002, and Nolene was excited.

But the ship soon sprang a leak. Nolene had started getting drunk almost every evening. Initially I chose to ignore it. Then, two weeks before our wedding, we got into a huge fight when she said I had accused her of wanting to marry me so that she could get a South African passport. I should have run for the hills then and never looked back. I hadn't even realised I was her ticket to South African residency! My guides had shown themselves to me more than once in this period with Nolene, but I had ignored them. Now they were going to give me a lesson of note.

The morning after our argument, after a tense silence, I overheard her calling her friends, telling them what an arsehole she was marrying. I actually had murderous thoughts. The next minute she was all over me with, 'You mean the world to me.' She was acting the victim, appealing to my soft, sensitive side. She was a drunk and *I* was apologising. But Nolene was a manipulator: I was the bully in this scene.

The gods were deliberately placing obstacles in my way, which I chose to ignore. Her family couldn't be at the wedding, and neither could my sister, who was writing exams in Johannesburg. But Nolene was adamant that we could not postpone the wedding; under duress, I allowed the plans to go ahead for October. We decided on having a beach wedding, attended by a small number of intimate friends, followed by drinks and a reception at a nearby restaurant.

The day arrived for the Blouberg beach ceremony. The weatherman had predicted a cloudless sky. As I drove towards the location, I could see the horizon darkening by the minute. By the time I got to the beach, the wind was howling. Was it me or the weatherman who had the days mixed up? It wasn't a good day for a beach walk, never mind a beach wedding. Again the gods were shouting – but again I did not listen.

My best man and I walked down to the beach and stood chatting for what seemed like hours. Nerves and weather certainly played a part here. I then heard music in the distance – not our 'wedding march', so we carried on chatting. I casually turned around, only to see Nolene walking towards me, a look of enquiry on her face. I must have looked pretty shocked too.

The plan had been for Nolene to make her entrance down the steps of the promenade to the music we had chosen – the first part of 'Minstrel Boy', an instrumental piece by the Irish group, The Corrs. We had paced out the route and practised the procession.

Unbeknown to me, my wonderful future wife had switched the song. Walking down the 'aisle', I found myself listening to a Whitney Houston number I'd never heard before. From the moment the bride had arrived at my side, I'd wished for the courage to leave the beach. Instead, we were married.

Twenty-four hours later, the fact that I had messed up her entrance was thrown in my face. *I* had fucked up again: it had been my fault entirely and, as per usual, *I* had not listened.

After the ceremony, we walked up to the restaurant and

toasted our marriage with a few speeches. Then we drove off to another restaurant on the other side of town, where our friends were waiting.

We had our first dance as a married couple for the benefit of the wedding guests, forcing a smile to save face. 'Isn't it supposed to be one of the happiest days of my life?' I wondered. Instead, I felt like I was beginning a life sentence. Afterwards, we mingled with the guests. Nolene wanted me to ask the disc jockey to play a specific song so that she could dance with her friend Jimmy, who had introduced us. Amid the noise, the disc jockey did not hear me clearly, so he played the wrong song.

Nolene stormed over. 'Can't you do a fucking thing right?' she screamed at me.

What had I done? Who was this woman with whom I was going to spend the rest of my life with? Nolene danced the rest of the evening away – on her own. She became increasingly drunk and, at midnight, passed out. Fortunately most of the guests had already left, and the few stragglers didn't notice her. I tumbled her into the car with the help of a friend. I was exhausted – both emotionally and physically.

Somehow we got through the weekend, and I put the wedding and the reception behind me. Due to Nolene's work commitments, we had put off our honeymoon.

There was another huge warning sign on the Monday – only four days after our 'big day'. Nolene had been seeing a psychologist for close to a year prior to our meeting.

She came home that evening after a session and told me, 'My therapist says that you are the cause of my nightmares.'

'Am I superhuman? Creating nightmares in the brains of others?' I questioned, flabbergasted. People have said that I have healing powers, but this was beyond me. Nolene poured another gin and tonic – the best depressant, the solution to all problems.

Our discussion ended in a screaming match. It's impossible to reason with an inebriated person, so I retreated to the spare bedroom to gather my thoughts.

And so our marriage lasted all of four days – one of the shortest marriages in history? It was over before it had even started. I blamed myself for tolerating her abuse. But why had I moved to the spare bedroom instead of walking out the front door? I knew I should have left, but what would my family and friends have thought? Again, I had failed in a relationship. I was too embarrassed to acknowledge that I had made a huge mistake. How had I allowed this marriage to happen? Could it be saved? I thought I should at least try. Also, I thought I loved the woman.

For the next month, we acknowledged each other in the passageway (I was still sleeping in the spare bedroom). I believe Nolene actually enjoyed this period. She didn't have to talk to me and she could drink as much as she liked.

Shortly after we started the 'separation', she told me that she had been doing some reading and had ascertained where my problems lay. It is always amazing to me that we are so good at diagnosing others' faults.

'You are suffering from ADHD (attention deficit hyperactivity disorder). This is the cause of the problems in our marriage, and you must go for help as soon as possible.'

According to 'Dr Nolene', I'd had the syndrome all my life, and now she had managed to diagnose it correctly.

'Go and read up on Klinefelter's syndrome,' I responded.

But she persisted: 'A psychiatrist can prescribe Ritalin. Once you're on medication, you'll begin to behave like a normal human being.'

I actually considered it for a moment! Then my rational side took over – what was I thinking? Why could Nolene not just admit that she had made a mistake? That she didn't love me and wanted out? Ah – the passport.

I was so tired of arguing that I said I would sleep on it. But I had no intention of thinking about it. I was an adult and there was no way that I was about to take Ritalin. The next morning, I told Nolene that I would go and see a psychiatrist. I just wanted to prove her wrong, though I certainly didn't tell her that! The look of triumph and satisfaction on her face almost made me change my mind. But the turning point came when I phoned the psychiatrist: a session would cost double the going rate. In my head, I told them both to get stuffed. If I was going to spend any of my money, it would be on marriage counselling for both of us.

The ranting and raving started all over again. I was told that I was an idiot; I should walk around with a sign on my forehead that read 'dangerous'; I was a menace.

A month later, Nolene announced that her ex-boyfriend in England had offered her a job for two months. She tried to convince me that accepting the offer would be good for our future.

'It's bad timing,' I said. 'I believe that our marriage should come first.'

But Nolene insisted that everything would be fine and, before I could protest, she phoned her ex to tell him that she'd fly over the next week.

We spent our last evening together at a restaurant in town. I had wanted to spend the time alone with her – I was still hoping we could save the marriage – but as we sat down, she greeted two friends she recognised and insisted they join us. Again my suspicions were confirmed: all I was providing was the passport.

Somehow the distance between us helped. We spoke every day. While she was in England, she stayed with her sister in an alcohol-free house. I was talking to a sober person. I guess this, and the truth of the old saying 'absence makes the heart grow fonder', led me to look forward to seeing her again.

One evening I phoned and a different Nolene picked up. I presumed she was tired and still working, and asked, 'Where are you?' She evaded the question. Then she told me she was having dinner with her ex. My gut was telling me that they were sleeping together. It turned out that she would rather be with a man who had messed her around and broken her heart than work on our relationship.

Nolene flew back the day before Christmas. She did not allow me to hug her. 'Don't hug me here, in public, at the airport,' she said.

I was dumbfounded, but remembered the real Nolene – no emotion to be shown, especially not in public. When we got home, she continued to resist any displays of affection.

'Just leave me alone,' she grumbled. 'I'm exhausted. I want to go to sleep.'

In the morning, she woke up having had a brainwave. She wanted to invite all her friends round for Christmas lunch.

'Can't we enjoy a quiet day together?' I asked.

But no, Nolene won again and we had all her friends round.

By mid-afternoon, she was smashed. I'm not sure why it upset me so much. Had I been naive to hope that she might have changed in England?

Once everybody had left, we again got into one of our stupid arguments. This time it was about women's magazines. She had bought quite a few magazines at the airport – they were expensive – and I made a comment that got blown way out of proportion, to the extent that Nolene asked me to move out of the house.

'On the first of January,' she demanded. Then she changed her mind and said it could be the second. She must have been thinking she was doing me a favour. A part of me was relieved: the abuse would finally be over. In the New Year I moved out and she got a housemate.

Nolene took on another three-month contract in the United Kingdom. Her master plan was on schedule – anything to be as far away as possible from the person she had married.

I was still giving our mutual friend, Jimmy, shiatsu treatments. He was my closest link to Nolene, knew my feelings for her, and had been a good friend to me when we were having problems. One day he told me that Home Affairs had turned down Nolene's application for residency.

He paused. 'Can you help her?'

The bloody passport! The anger boiled inside me, and yet my heart was breaking. My head told me to laugh it off, but my heart overruled it: I would help the bitch get her passport. I gritted my milk teeth as I drove away from Jimmy's house, my head a jumble of thoughts. I could never understand how people could stay in abusive relationships, how they didn't have the courage to move on. How ironic – now here I was, in the same situation. Was this not emotional abuse I was experiencing?

An hour later Nolene phoned. I told her I would help her, and I could almost feel her relief down the telephone line. I asked her if we could meet for tea or even dinner, but was rewarded with dead silence. She was as cold as ice – this was business. 'Maybe afterwards, Stephen. I need to sort this out first.' Her whole conversation sounded rehearsed. We made an appoinment at Home Affairs for the next day. That night I battled to sleep, tossing and turning, doubting my decision to help her. But Nolene probably had the best night's sleep she'd had in a long time, knowing that she had finally got this sucker to help her accomplish her goal.

The next day, I left work and drove up to her place. Although the journey normally took about half an hour, on that day it seemed to take forever. I drove up the driveway and Nolene was waiting at the front door, looking smug. How I wished that I was stronger and could tell her to go and fuck herself. But that soft, ridiculous side of me took over again. Nolene gave me a half-hearted, obligatory hug.

The next moment she was all business. Coffee was offered as a courtesy. I didn't have a voice. This woman should have gone to war – no reason to send all our men. She was a real toughie.

But, during our drive to Home Affairs, Nolene and I chatted as if we were dating. She was suddenly so sweet: laughing, joking and just being happy. It was the Nolene she reserved for her friends. She played her role to perfection – no rehearsal. She sat next to me as we faced one of the Home Affairs officers and held my hand, telling them, 'We want to live together and be happy without me having to go out of the country all the time to renew my visa.'

She was so convincing, even I was starting to believe her.

We answered all the officials' questions. They also required proof, in the form of an affidavit from my mother, to say that she knew we had been dating for the past couple of years. I had to lie and – the worst part – I made my mother lie. I couldn't believe I was doing it.

On the way back home, ever hopeful, I suggested that perhaps we could go back to dating and try again. Nolene's mood turned black – I'd been fooled again. She had put in another Oscar-winning performance. She again suggested that I seek psychological help for my supposed ADHD – she was playing doctor again.

I had lied for her. I pride myself on not being a liar, but now I had lied to the authorities *and* implicated my mother. And Nolene had happily watched me lie on her behalf. I felt like a fool. I also longed to talk openly to an unbiased person. I started sleeping badly.

Eventually I approached a priest. Perhaps he could offer solace or even a solution? I wanted him to tell me that I had made a terrible mistake.

All I got was, 'God is with you.'

I sat open-mouthed, shocked. 'Is this all a priest can offer? No compassion?' I asked myself. Then the penny dropped – the only person who could tell me anything was me. At last I understood that only *I* knew the answers to my problems.

Nolene went back to England to work again. After a month or so, she returned. I asked her to meet me for dinner – choosing a public place, rather than meeting her on her territory. I was not happy about the lies we had told to Home Affairs – I felt we should really try to make the marriage work.

The day leading up to our date dragged on – the knot in my

stomach increased hourly. I just wanted the evening to be over. I visualised the following day – after the grand finale – feeling as if a weight had been lifted from my shoulders. Eventually 7 p.m. arrived. 'Will I be able to eat a meal?' I worried.

At the restaurant I waited ten minutes for Madame. I was being generous – I was allowing her to play her little games. When she arrived, she pecked me on the cheek.

I asked the waiter to leave us with our menus for a few minutes and indulged in a bit of small talk – enquiring about England, her family, and so on.

She eventually asked, 'Why this dinner?'

I stalled. We continued chatting about this and that until our food arrived. Nolene asked me the odd question about my life, although she didn't listen to my response. I could feel the sweat running down my forehead.

Finally, I could bear it no longer and said: 'Nolene, my heart tells me I am in love with you. My head tells me we are being dishonest. I can't go through with this any more.'

'My father is ill,' Nolene said. 'I need to go to England regularly to care for him.'

'But our marriage is a farce,' I protested.

'He's old. And I promise to come back.'

I waited. Her mind was working overtime. I challenged her again. What was her response? Emotional blackmail. She begged me to help her, citing her sick, elderly father and her filial love. I couldn't see what that had to do with our relationship. When it became clear that I wasn't falling for her story, she started cursing me, calling me 'a prick, an arsehole and a weak, ineffectual specimen'. Her face had turned bright red. I thought she was going to burst a blood vessel, or even have heart failure. Eventually she got up, threw money on the table, glared at me one last time, and stormed off. I sat there, too embarrassed and stunned to move. Other patrons stared at me – I felt like a total idiot. I tried to find a good time to leave, but there was no right moment in a situation such as this. After some time had elapsed, I settled the bill and, my composure somewhat restored, quietly left.

Talk about being a sucker: two days later I called her. Every voice in my head was screaming, 'No – don't do it!' When she answered the phone, I begged, I pleaded, I grovelled. Finally I put the phone down. For the first time in ages, I broke down and cried ... and cried. Tears for losing this woman whom I so desperately wanted; tears over my lack of self-esteem and why I couldn't stop myself from seeking the abuse.

A week later, Jimmy took me out for coffee and asked me to reconsider the passport issue. He gave me another sob story: how Nolene would have to put her dogs down if she couldn't get her South African passport. It was a cleverly plotted move. Nolene knew I had a soft spot for animals. And so I agreed to stay married to my precious wife. She would get her piece of paper.

On 7 June 2003, my birthday, I waited to hear from her. Nothing – not even a phone call. Although I have never been big on birthday bashes, I did expect an acknowledgement of some sort. Nolene had cooked her own goose. The next day, I consulted an attorney and started divorce proceedings. My attorney suggested that we consult an advocate.

'Your wife is not a resident of this country and the proceedings could become tricky,' he explained.

When we saw the advocate, he told me, 'You have been suckered good and proper.'

I needed to hear it from somebody else. Finally I had made the right decision.

The attorney said we had to get the timing right. His office had to issue the summons to Nolene in between her UK visits. Fighting the matter in both the London and Cape Town High Courts would be too complicated and costly.

The advocate explained: 'I don't generally do this … it's considered a dirty move. But you've really had the wool pulled over your eyes.'

To ensure that Nolene didn't 'get away', they called her home on a daily basis. They spun her housemate a yarn about being property agents doing a survey and said they had to speak to the leaseholder urgently. In this way they found out the date of her return.

The day finally came when the attorneys would issue the summons – a few days before Nolene was due to leave South Africa, the sheriff of the court served the summons and made her sign for the receipt. She had no time to consult a lawyer. I would have loved to have been a fly on the wall. My abuser had suddenly had the wind knocked out of her sails.

Nolene contested the divorce on the grounds that I was 'after her money'; apparently she had money stashed away in England. Looking back, I recall that each time she had had too much to drink, she accused me of being a gold-digger. Now the accusation made sense, though I have no idea whether she actually had any money or not.

Our divorce was finalised on 21 July 2003. This ordeal would take another two years to sort out emotionally, but it was the best cosmic shake-up ever.

24

Findhorn

I was miserable being on my own. I had failed at marriage, and it hurt. I had tried hard with every relationship, but each one had taken something out of me. I longed for love and a true meeting of two souls. And I wanted to be accepted for who I was. I slunk away from the marriage and retired to my own space, where I licked my wounds.

Then my luck changed – my sister offered to sponsor a trip to Scotland in June 2005: a trip back to the country I loved and a chance to visit Findhorn. Friends had sung the praises of this spiritual community in the north-east of Scotland, known for growing gigantic cabbages. I had read up about it. Findhorn offered courses in communal and spiritual living, and new paradigms of living in harmony with the planet. I longed for something that would change *my* status quo and I yearned to feel the community's spiritual essence.

Findhorn is situated on a bay some thirty kilometres from Inverness, close to the outskirts of a small town, Forres. I booked to attend one of their courses, open to experiencing adventure and the challenges it presented. I had never travelled overseas without someone waiting to welcome me on the other side, and had panic attacks just thinking about it. I was tempted to cancel the trip, yet I felt a deep need to experience Findhorn. Leaving South Africa was the easy part. Having nobody waiting for me in the United Kingdom was the scary bit.

I arrived in Forres – an old northern Scottish town of grey

granite and cobbled streets – late one afternoon. I could not see any bus stop or taxi rank. The streets were quiet and mostly deserted. I lugged my backpack up the street with no idea which direction I should take. I was taking responsibility for my own destiny. I walked right across town with the heavy pack looking for a guest house.

Tired from the long flights, it felt as if the pack weighed a ton, although I had packed lightly. By now the sun had already set and I began to consider sleeping among the cows in a near-by field. But as I approached the edge of the town, I saw a small B&B opposite a Sainsbury's supermarket. Fortunately, there had been a cancellation. The landlady quoted me thirty pounds for the night. I asked if she could drop the amount to twenty.

'Twenty-five pounds,' she said. 'You are welcome to stay the night and I'll cook you a fry-up in the morning.'

The double-storey B&B had three guest rooms, each with a small handbasin, a fridge and a television set. There was a shared bathroom at the end of the passage. The view from my bedroom window featured a glass conservatory.

After settling in, I walked back into the town in search of a meal. Forres is famous for being the home of the Benromach distillery. I have a weakness for a good whisky, particularly malts. Benromach produced a few. The distillery was still open. I took the tour, learning more about the processes and pleasures of whisky, and afterwards purchased a bottle of their finest – I should have bought two! Then I continued my short walk, as it was a small town. I wondered about the people who might never have seen another town, who were born and destined to die here. Eventually I found a pub and ordered a pie with gravy. Then, jet-lagged, I crawled back to the guest house and got into bed.

The next morning I took a bus to the village of Findhorn, enjoying the ride through the green countryside. I imagined it was green for most of the year. Driving along the coast, I was reminded of the Cape coastal scenery, but here there was heather and other foreign-looking plants that grew happily in the salty marshes. It was a short five-mile trip to Findhorn. The bus drove around the bay of Moray past an airbase, pulling up to a picnic site.

There, the driver announced, 'Findhorn.'

I did a double take. 'He must be mistaken,' I thought. The place looked like a caravan park, or a place to have picnics. I was stunned. Was this the mysterious place that had sprung to fame in the 1960s for its alternative philosophy and gigantic cabbages? I had imagined a much more structured environment, not a sleepy holiday camp. With misgivings I got off the bus.

I walked up the pathway to the camp. A few people were busy working in the vegetable patch. No giant cabbages there, only long-haired, tatty-looking gardeners. A couple rode past on bicycles. Someone was sitting under a tree in a meditative pose. These folk were reminiscent of a past era. They all looked like hippies. Was I in Woodstock, back in 1969? 'Maybe I should turn tail and run,' I panicked. Common sense prevailed, however. I hadn't travelled all this way to be put off by a few off-the-wall, weirdly dressed people.

The tiny office was a combination of canteen and bookshop. The woman behind the counter told me registration took place in the community centre in the park. I proceeded there along a road lined with caravans, small houses and tall pine trees.

A collection of small, round Hobbit-like houses dotted the landscape. I could see a building project was on the go and the building materials were straw bales and mud – they were cob houses. I came to a big, wooden, dome-like structure with a carved sign reading: 'Community Centre'. Inside was a kitchen and a large communal dining hall.

The promotional literature described Findhorn as a place where one could feel at peace and get in touch with one's inner self. The community was founded in 1962 by Eileen and Peter Caddy and Dorothy Mclean. They had given up a secure livelihood in order to lead a more spiritual existence, listening to their inner guidance. Dorothy found that she could contact the spirit, or *deva*, of plants, so she began to communicate with the vegetables. I know it sounds like hogwash; it initially did to me too.

I was at Findhorn to participate in what they called 'Experience Week'. All first-timers are required to undertake this one-week group experience, an introduction to the philosophy and life of Findhorn. I met the people sharing my week: twelve women and three men, ranging in age from nineteen to sixty. Our facilitators divided us into teams and allotted each team a house. This was to be my home for the next ten days. I shared mine with five others from different parts of the world: a husband-and-wife team and a young girl, all from Canada, an Englishman, and a woman from New Zealand. Encountering such a variety of nationalities was a learning curve in itself.

I was scared, nervous and excited, all at the same time. Was this perhaps a new beginning for me?

The air force base I had passed that morning was only five miles away from our house. We could hear the jets taking off and landing at all hours of the night. It seemed such a contradiction to the quiet, idyllic life we were leading.

Findhorn is almost completely self-sufficient. The morning after our registration we were given a choice of jobs to do that would pay our way (similar to the ways of a kibbutz): working either in the garden, with its healthy crop of vegetables that fed the community, or in the kitchen, cooking food for 250 people every day. I chose to work in the kitchen purely because it was raining half the time. Five of us cooked. It was quite a task to decide how many potatoes or carrots to peel for so many people! The kitchen was equipped with all the mod cons, including a large washing area and catering-sized gas stoves.

The Australians I worked with loved Johnny Clegg. Johnny will never know how popular he was up there in Scotland! In the mornings, we met in the big hall – known as the Universal Hall – for what the community calls 'attunement'. Everyone stands in a circle with their eyes closed, holding hands. They invoke the angel of the day, or the angel of the activity they are busy with, and ask for a blessing. If there are any problems or unresolved issues between people, these are discussed and resolved then and there. All the programmes are 'attuned' to being aware.

Besides working in the kitchen, we were also led through a range of self-discovery exercises. We danced to lovely but unusual music, during which we each got in touch with our inner child. We played a 'trust game' in which, blindfolded, we had to allow a partner to lead us around obstacles: we had to learn to trust again.

At first I thought these games were ridiculous. But once I

realised the others were also struggling, I let go of my inhibitions.

We also went on outings to explore the surrounding area. The forests were filled with gigantic oak and fir trees covered with lichen and old man's beard. It was interesting to see trees, which I normally only saw in public parks in South Africa, growing wild along the riverbanks. At a place in the forest called Randolph's Leap we were told some local myths and of the mysteries of Druid life. We would walk in the forest and along the rivers, listening, smelling and observing.

One of my favourite walks meandered for two kilometres from the camp to the ocean. The beach was rough, covered in stones and broken seashells. Along the length of it stood concrete blockhouses dating back to the Second World War. On the water's edge, they had been built in the late 1930s to safeguard the coastline against a German invasion.

For a few days while I was at Findhorn the temperature rose to 25° C – a heatwave for Scotland. All the locals, with their lily-white skins, were frolicking in the water, despite its sub-zero temperature.

Afternoons were allocated to work, while the evenings were our quiet times. We could visit the other houses to chat about the events of the day. Some people would become tearful as they offloaded their issues; others remained silent and contemplative. Halfway through the retreat, in a beautiful quiet space, I made the decision to write this book. I knew that in order to heal fully, I would have to mend myself. Before I could practise as a healer, or be fully present in a relationship, I had to be whole. Writing my story would help me come to terms with my issues and aid the healing process.

I had already begun to realise certain things – in the groups and during the exercises I saw that I was accepted. People liked me. I knew I was a nice person and that, even though I had problems, I wasn't the only one. Everyone else has problems too. They might not have the challenges I have had with the extra x, but they have their own trials. At Findhorn I stopped feeling sorry for myself and viewing myself as a victim. Instead, I started realising that having the extra x allowed me to be a more empathetic person. I was someone who was in touch with his feelings and who could relate well to others. The testosterone had helped me to experience my manhood almost like any normal man, but I had the added advantage of increased empathy, thanks to that extra x. I could be useful by helping others with my syndrome to understand it and come to terms with their condition.

Just before the end of my two-week stay, I was chatting to an English friend, Kim. She told me she wanted to write a book about her life. It was quiet around us while I listened to her – the afternoon sun was going down and rabbits had come from the hedgerows to nibble on the grass.

'I have also felt that I should write a book about *my* life,' I said.

She looked puzzled, and I told her about Klinefelter's syndrome. She listened intently and then said, with absolute certainty, that I should write my story. Perhaps it was our conversation or perhaps just the tranquil afternoon but, for the next couple of days, writing the book was all I could think about.

Everyone had told me that people have revelations up at Findhorn. I had just had mine.

I told the others, and they encouraged me, saying that I

should talk about my syndrome in order to perhaps help others. My two weeks had passed all too quickly. I was sad to say goodbye, as we had shared our lives with each other in such a short space of time. Of course, we all promised to stay in touch, but such promises eventually tend to fall by the wayside. For a while I wrote to two members of the group, but, eventually, having got what I needed from the experience, the time had arrived for me to apply the principles to my life.

25

Purple and orange flashes

Tina came into my life quite by chance – in between purple and orange flashes and an eye op. Perhaps she had come to open my eyes? I had been single for about two years and was quite enjoying my freedom. One evening I invited some friends, Jill and Peter, to dinner.

During the dinner, Jill said, 'You are so like my friend Tina. Everything is so tidy. You should really meet her.'

A few weeks later, Jill and Peter invited me for a meal. Unbeknown to me, it had been Tina's suggestion. She wanted to meet the guy who kept his things so neatly organised. They suggested we have Christmas Eve dinner together – Tina would do most of the cooking.

I arrived early (as usual), feeling nervy, being in new and unknown territory. About half an hour later, in walked a woman with beautiful legs. Tina is tall and very slender, with a fantastic figure, blue eyes, and reddish-brown hair. We were introduced. I felt awkward; this girl had attitude. I was self-conscious and even a little afraid. My heart was aflutter, but could I trust it after the disasters of previous relationships? Tina and I started chatting and I felt a warmth towards her. She was a good conversationalist, but I struggled through the evening and was relieved when it finally came to an end.

Our second meeting, a couple of days later, was more casual: an evening of playing cards. Tina had arranged it – a foursome. What was I worried about? I wanted to get to know this person better, but I had to tread very lightly. I was intrigued by Tina, but my bad experiences still loomed large in my mind. Also, I wanted to write my book. I decided to slow down.

But I kept thinking about Tina, still wanting to take her out. When I finally called, suggesting dinner, she said, 'Why don't you come over to my house instead?'

We made an arrangement for the Friday evening. She asked if there was anything I didn't eat, and I said 'onions'.

Tina's house was a quaint semi, the front door set right on the street, which leads down a long passage to a big lounge and a dining room at the back. Here, double French doors opened onto the rear garden. Tina had painted the horrible precast walls a lovely blue.

Everything in the garden seemed to jump out at me, the greens seeming much brighter than usual. Tina pointed out the trees – tall ficus and quiver. I sensed she was just as nervous as I was. We had a glass of wine under the stars and chatted away. I found Tina to be a lot more relaxed on her own. Eventually we sat down to eat – Tina had made a delicious chicken dish. Unfortunately the chicken was on the bone, which was not my favourite, but she didn't know that – I'd said it was only onions I didn't eat! It was only much later on that she revealed she'd guessed this, by the way I had picked at my food. We had a laugh about it.

After that evening, we started to date seriously, but it wasn't an easy road. In the early days, for about three months, we saw each other only on weekends. Then Tina decided to end our relationship – she wasn't sure about us and thought it best if we split up. Naturally I was confused and upset, as we had been getting on so well. But after a few days Tina called and we started to talk on the telephone daily once again. Then we started dating again. After a month of dating, she wanted to split up again!

During that split, I briefly dated another woman, Darcy. After being together for a month, I decided to tell her that I had Klinefelter's syndrome. Darcy listened, but said nothing. The next day she said she couldn't be with me any more – she needed time to think. She left without another word, and I heard nothing from her for the next three days.

I decided to give Tina a call. I let the phone ring for about fifteen seconds before I asked myself what I was doing.

About an hour later Tina called me, asking whether I had tried to get hold of her. We ended up talking for five hours. I could hear her crying.

'What's the problem?' I asked.

'We should talk face to face,' she said.

We decided that I would visit her at her house the following evening. I had missed her the whole time we had been apart and I could feel the twinge of excitement again. As I was about to leave for Tina's, Darcy called me, saying she realised she had made a mistake. She asked if we could meet the next Friday night. Like a fool, I agreed.

Tina and I spoke for hours at her house. We both admitted that we still had feelings for each other and ended up sleeping together. Afterwards, I knew I could never go back to Darcy. I told Tina that I had a date with Darcy on the Friday evening, but that I'd tell her that night that I couldn't see her again.

I picked Darcy up at her house. She placed a kiss on my cheek as I let her into the car and remarked that I had a very worried look on my face. She asked me what was wrong. I spluttered and eventually told her that I was going back to Tina, and that I was sorry for the way things had worked out. At first she was silent, but then she suddenly said that I was a bastard.

'But you were the one who walked out on me, and not the other way round,' I reminded her.

'Please stop the car so that I can walk home,' she said.

I should just have cancelled the dinner before, I guess. I turned the car around and drove Darcy home.

Then I drove over to Tina's and told her what had happened, feeling bad about it all. The thing I liked about Tina was her straightforwardness and honesty. She told me to stop being stupid. I looked at her. I loved this woman – her cocky spirit, her bright blue eyes. And we had so much in common. One bizarre shared interest is that we both like visiting old graveyards. We were a match made in heaven!

Tina had come into my life at just the right time. When we'd first met I'd asked her what she liked – her favourite colour and other stupid things. Her reply was, 'Is this Twenty Questions?' I later explained that I'd felt awkward because I didn't know anyone in the room.

I first mentioned Klinefelter's syndrome to Tina that same night – the one on which we met. She had asked me what I was doing in my life work-wise, and I told her that I was writing a book about myself. She looked at me oddly.

Much later on, Tina told me that she had thought, 'This guy is really full of himself.'

Tina does not want to have children. Her ex-husband had a child from a previous relationship, but she chose consciously not to have any kids of her own. It was never an issue, and so, later on, when I told her that I was sterile, she just shrugged and smiled.

When I'd returned from Scotland, I started working for a friend who had a business in pool safety nets – my job was to drop off his company's pamphlets at various pool shops. This, together with the odd shiatsu treatment, kept the wolf from the door. Then, in October 2005, I was employed full time to assess the pools of potential clients. I took measurements and did checks to prevent major hitches. Occasionally, I would help with the trickier installations.

The end of November brought another day to forget. I was at a client's house to take measurements for a pool net. I went down the side of the house with the client's son to the back-yard and noticed a pole jutting out of a makeshift washing line. I registered: 'Be careful of that when you come back.' I stooped down (I am six foot two) to walk underneath the pole. I measured the pool, made my notes and stood up.

A sudden pain shot through the side of my head. Had some-body hit me? I tasted blood – a warm trickle ran down my face. I couldn't see; everything was a blur. I had walked into another pole, one I hadn't seen. It had struck me on the side of my face, missing my left eye by millimetres. My glasses broke on impact; the left lens cracked right through.

The client helped to clean me up. Wiping away the blood, I saw a large gash running across my nose and left cheek. Having put tissue paper on the gash to stop the bleeding, I went to see an optician. As the army doctor discovered all those years ago, I am bat-blind without my specs.

'You'll have to wait until January 2006 to get new glasses,' was the news. 'The lenses have to be imported from Israel.'

Back to my old glasses. Better than nothing, I suppose.

Two days later, I cycled off at 4.30 a.m. It's a wonderful time of the morning: no traffic, and I get to work on time. Cycling through an unlit area, I noticed streaks of light to the side of me. Was my mind playing tricks? I was cycling right under some power lines. Did it have something to do with the electricity? A few kilometres further, the flashing started again.

I realised it was coming from my right eye.

I rode the last thirty kilometres home, and later that morning I contacted my doctor.

'What's wrong?' she asked me. My gut told me a detached retina, which I mentioned to the doctor. She agreed that it was possible and gave me another doctor's name, urging, 'See this eye specialist right away. He's the best in his field.'

The best was out of town. His receptionist gave me another expert's number, and the new specialist squeezed me in. During the examination, he dilated the pupil so that he could see the back area of my eye.

'Have you been bungee jumping? Taken a knock to your head?'

He diagnosed that the gel in the eye had dislodged. 'It is causing the flashes of light – what we call "floaters".'

Every time I blinked, I saw the little dots.

'Best to leave it for a while,' he advised. 'Come back in two weeks. If the floaters increase or become worse, an operation will be necessary.'

Poor Tina. By now, she was very much a part of my life and of the eye drama. Once again my fears surfaced: I was a wreck, feeling vulnerable and needing help. Would she be able to cope?

Every time I drove, I could see only half the road. I eventually contacted the specialist.

'It's a fairly simple op,' he reassured me. 'The procedure takes about three hours. General anaesthetic. I'll insert needles above and below the eye. One of the needles sucks the gel out of the eye, the second will blow air into the eye to keep the shape, and the third will pump the solution into the eye.'

I was shaky. My previous experience with an eye operation had been disastrous. However, all seemed to go well during the operation. The specialist discharged me afterwards and I was able to go home wearing an eyepatch – every little boy's dream. Tina drove me back to her house. Not being totally mobile and a bit out of sorts, I ended up spending the next two weeks there. The doctor had booked me off work for ten days.

Once at Tina's, I passed out, to wake only later, in the early part of the evening. I was still feeling a bit woozy from the anaesthetic and wanted a bath before collapsing into bed. As I bent over the bath to let in the water, I suddenly felt a thud at the back of my head and beautiful colours emerged in front of my eyes – bright purples and oranges that looked like flowers.

Tina entered the room and I looked at her through the bouquet of flowers. Purple and orange suited her. I smiled. It's bizarre, but I was actually enjoying the vision. She looked so beautiful that I wanted to suspend time – I wanted to go on seeing the amazing colours and this remarkable woman. Perhaps it was an omen so that I could see Tina in her true colours. She was lovely.

But Tina was concerned. 'Did you hit your head on anything?'

'No.'

Was it perhaps a side effect from the anaesthetic? I realised something was amiss. Too many botched operations, I thought. But I nevertheless got on with my bath. Maybe the colours would be gone by morning.

The next morning, Tina took me to the clinic. The eye surgeon removed the dressings and looked at my eye.

'It's a blood clot, that's what's causing the trouble.'

I tried to see with the eye, but there was only darkness.

'Once the blood clot has disintegrated, everything will be fine,' the surgeon reassured me. 'Give it a couple of days. The operation has been a success.'

For whom? I pondered these words that I had heard so many times in my life.

The surgeon gave me drops, saying, 'See me in a few days.'

I was in a huge panic, but I had to take his word for it. I couldn't imagine having the use of only one eye for the rest of my life. Fortunately, the problem corrected itself over the next two – very long – weeks.

Tina and I settled into a loving and warm relationship. As had been the case so often in my relationships, I had suffered a trauma as its outset. But Tina had helped me through the purple and orange psychedelic flowers and the eye op. She is a feisty and headstrong woman, but she has also proved to be affectionate and nurturing. I was beginning to learn to leave the memories of abuse and trauma behind me and trust that the universe was good and kind. Tina helped show me the way.

26

A stash of sweets

September 2006: what would happen next in the life of Stephen, the Klinefelter's Kid? My mother, who was about to turn seventy-six, still ate sweets with the vigour of a five-year-old. Diagnosed in her mid-forties with diabetes, she kept telling us, her children, 'My diabetes is different from the diagnoses of other people.' She was in complete denial, and we were not able to get our stubborn mother to change.

'But I am a bit concerned about my feet,' she admitted. This time there was a note of urgency in her voice. 'I can hardly stand, let alone walk.'

She had developed sores on her legs, which had turned into open wounds. They had also increased in size to about the diameter of a ten-cent piece. Her self-diagnosis?

'Probably some kind of rash.'

I had studied anatomy as part of my shiatsu training. Looking at her feet, I immediately thought, 'Some rash! You have to be kidding – it's the beginning of gangrene!' Her toes were black.

'Mom, you have to have this checked out,' I insisted.

She finally gave in and saw a doctor, who immediately referred her to a surgeon. Diagnosis? Gangrene on her big toe and the toe next to it; they needed to amputate both digits before the gangrene spread. Mom was admitted to hospital the following week.

Christine, Johnny and I tried to reassure her. Christine flew to Cape Town from Johannesburg – she wanted to be with Mom as she came round. In the doctor's eyes, the operation was a success. When Mom awoke, she muttered, 'Strange. I'm not in much pain.'

The doctor said, 'The toes literally fell off.'

During Mom's stay in hospital, we cleared her cupboards of all 'no-no' foods. We could have opened our own sweet shop with what she had stashed. We were treating her like a child, but we'd decided that a change in her eating patterns might keep her with us a while longer.

Eventually, Mom seemed to be on the road to recovery. But suddenly she complained of excruciating pain in her leg. The doctors announced the spread of the gangrene: 'We have to amputate just below the knee.'

This second amputation would allow a prosthesis to be fitted. The theatre was booked for the next day.

That evening was the most intimate time I ever spent with my mother. I think those moments were so special because, in my heart, I knew that she would not be with us for much longer. We talked about everyday life, and about medical matters, and where we thought we would go after we died. We found common ground. But in my heart I was angry – I wished she had taken better care of herself. It was as if she could read my mind because, just before I left the hospital, she suddenly fell quiet. A dead silence. It only lasted for about fifteen seconds, and then she said, 'I suppose I could have done something about this earlier on.'

I nodded.

'I'm really worried about the surgery tomorrow morning,' she admitted.

'Everything will be fine,' I assured her, but deep down I knew that this was pretty much the end.

She smiled at me. 'Yes,' she said. 'I'll be fine.'

I think she could sense that I was very worried.

I'll never forget that night. Would we ever have another moment like that? Although I was deeply concerned, I felt a sense of peace. I just wished the conversation could have lasted forever, but the hour was up all too soon. I left in tears. My mother and I had, over the years, become like best friends in our love–hate relationship. She often said I pushed her buttons. Likewise.

I tossed and turned the whole night, finally falling asleep in the early hours. At work that morning I awaited the dreaded call. Eventually, it came: 'The operation has been a success.'

Greatly relieved, I raced off to the hospital, my heart pounding. My mother lay peacefully in intensive care. When she came round, still doped, she mumbled, 'There's a lot of pain.'

I tried to reassure her. Christine again flew down from Johannesburg. The three of us took turns to go and see her so that there was always somebody at her bedside.

'There is a lot of activity at night,' Mom confided one evening. 'There were people landing outside in strange machines and taking the patients away. I swear blind that the person in the bed opposite mine has been taken by these machines.' (The patient she mentioned had been discharged.) Mom insisted that 'The staff have continual parties throughout the night.' The doctors explained that Mom's painkillers were causing her to hallucinate.

She would spend the next few days in intensive care before being transferred to a general ward. By then her skin tone and overall appearance had greatly improved. Her conversations were also more lucid, but she still complained of severe pain.

A physiotherapist came daily to exercise and thus increase the mobility of the other leg. My mother, being her stubborn self, would only wriggle her toes and then tell the physiotherapist, 'That's enough exercise for today.' These sessions only lasted about a half an hour – I don't think the physiotherapist could have handled her obstinacy for longer.

The doctors urged my mother to get out of bed, but she refused point-blank. We tried to tell her there was hope if she would just try. The doctors also tried to encourage her: 'The prosthesis will help you walk again.' But she just lay in that bed all day long.

Every now and then, her mind would slip and she would speak gibberish. She accused the physiotherapist, a man of twenty-five, of making a move on her. She suffered weeks of excruciating pain, and as her body was no longer fighting, the gangrene had spread. The doctors' solution to curb the infection was to amputate the leg above the knee. This would mean Mom spending the rest of her life in a wheelchair.

Christine, who had been flying back and forth weekly, came yet again for the third amputation. We tried to prepare ourselves. The body finds anaesthetic difficult to cope with at any age – never mind at seventy-six. Each operation, we assumed, would be the last.

We waited anxiously. But Mom was tougher than we'd thought and pulled through. Coming round, she started talking about her past and then reverted to gibberish; Mom was slowly losing her mind. After a few days in intensive care, she was sent back to the ward.

The physiotherapy started again. Christine and I helped the physiotherapist and told my mother, 'We won't drop you.

We'll hold on to you tightly. We have the strength to help you up.' But Mom would not trust us. Eventually, we let her be.

When Mom was ready to be discharged, we arranged for her to go to a rehabilitation centre, where they had more experience with amputees. My mother was nervous about leaving her safe space in hospital. Just before she left, a nurse asked me to collect her belongings, including her engagement and wedding rings. A ring of sentimental value – it had been my grandmother's engagement ring – was missing. Neither the nurses nor the cleaners knew anything about it. The ring was never found.

The rehabilitation centre was in an oval-shaped house. Each bedroom had two beds, and the window in Mom's room overlooked a small garden. The staff gave her a day to get used to the place, but on the second day they insisted that she start 'work'. Their biggest job was to get her to sit up so that they could move her into a wheelchair. Every afternoon after work, I went to see her. She had begun to look better, and for the first time in a long while, we managed to have coherent conversations.

But then she reverted to her old stubborn self and wanted to be left alone. I saw the same old story repeating itself. I tried to reason with her, but it was like hitting my head against a brick wall. Mother and son got into a shouting match.

'Just leave me alone.'

'Until you speak to me like a decent human being, I won't come to see you.'

She was beyond listening.

The tears ran down my cheeks as I drove home. I didn't go and see her for a couple of days. Christine was the healer of the rift. Mom had no recollection of the argument and asked, 'What is wrong with Stephen? Why doesn't he visit me?'

245

Eventually I went to see her again and we ended up crying together. In those few moments we shared, she seemed to be at peace. The conversation turned to old times and we laughed and joked. It was the last real conversation I had with my mother. I am glad it was a good one.

A week later Mom returned to the frail-care centre at the home for the elderly. Late that afternoon she had a massive stroke. The staff didn't even notice it. Christine and I found her with her mouth lopsided and her eye staring up at the ceiling. Back into hospital she had to go. The stroke had affected the left side of her body and her speech. She just lay there, staring into nothing. I spoke to her but got no response. Just silence. No recognition.

Each time I left the hospital after a visit, I wept. I phoned Christine daily. She was due to fly to the United States for a conference but cancelled her trip, even though the rest of her family had booked too, intending to meet her there. However, after much soul-searching, Christine eventually decided to go with the family. There was little she could do with my mother in a semi-coma anyway. But she flew to Cape Town one last time to see Mom, who managed to mumble a few words. Johnny was there too. We gathered that she was scared of going to the 'other side'.

Her three children told her, 'Let go. God is waiting for you.'

Christine kept telling her, 'There is a beautiful rose garden for you to tend.'

I sought the guidance of a priest – hoping he would have the words of comfort needed to make her transition easier.

But my mother held on, continuing to slip in and out of the coma. And then, finally, on Christmas morning, Mom passed away.

I felt a strange mix of relief and shock. I was happy that she was out of her pain and misery, but terribly sad to have lost a vital person in my life.

I was shown to her room for the last time. I lifted the sheet covering her face. She looked very tranquil; kind of happy. I was saying goodbye to a very special person – the one who had saved my life a long time ago when she insisted on walking me from doctor to doctor, persisting until I was correctly diagnosed with Klinefelter's. How I wish she had had the same dedication to her own well-being! But we all make choices in our lives, and she had made hers.

I was left to make the funeral arrangements, as Christine and Johnny were both away. Eventually Johnny returned from a holiday in Plettenberg Bay but, a week later, left for Zimbabwe. Whether the trip had been pre-planned, I will never know. There had been no mention of it. I felt they were taking advantage of me. Everybody seemed to be enjoying their Christmas vacation except for me, because I had to arrange the funeral. The death really hit me hard.

Mom had wanted to be buried next to my father in Johannesburg. I had no recollection of his grave's plot number, and had not visited the grave in the fifteen years I had lived in Cape Town. Fortunately, after many conversations with undertakers, and playing detective, we found the plot. But there was no space next to my dad's grave, so my mother had to be buried about half a kilometre away.

I thought the worst trauma was now over, but the real battle had only begun. I was left with the mammoth task of dealing with Mom's belongings. Although we thought we had cleared the flat of sweets, Tina and I were shocked at the amount we still found. They were hidden everywhere – in cupboards, between clothes, under the bed, in her bedside pedestal, even in empty suitcases. Most were well past their sell-by date. The clear-out added to my grief – I was distressed that Mom had so 'needed' these sweets that would eventually be the death of her.

Tina and I filled thirty bags with clothes for the Salvation Army. Some pieces still had the price tags on them, and others had long since ceased to fit her. We needed nearly two weeks to sort out mementos to give to family members.

A week into the sorting, my brother returned from Zimbabwe. We arranged to meet at the flat to sort out the financial papers. I intentionally arrived alone so we could discuss outstanding matters, but Johnny arrived with Val, his wife, in tow. As she came in, she voiced her likes and dislikes and listed what she wanted to take home. It was the final straw.

I let them have it: 'Where were you two when Tina and I were sorting out the flat? What gives you the right to waltz in here and demand goods?'

By the end of the afternoon I was so distressed that I told them, 'Take the lot. Just leave me the black-and-white photograph albums.'

They took what they wanted and didn't come back to help with the rest. Had my mother already been buried, she would have turned in her grave to hear us squabbling so. Val and I no longer talk unless we have to, and Tina and I are not invited to any social events she and Johnny host.

Then the day of the funeral: 17 January 2007. I would have been happier if Mom had been buried immediately, and had then had a memorial service. For me, the late burial delayed the grieving process. But, as always, I was outvoted and I shut my mouth.

27

Lungs, milk teeth and life lessons

Eleven months had passed following the death of my mother. It was November – a month when wind speeds reach forty knots or more in Cape Town. This November was no exception. Most winds in the Cape come from the south-east. Usually associated with dry weather, they are known to Capetonians as 'the Cape doctor'.

Sometimes rain is brought by 'black southeasters' and the sky darkens ominously, as if a thunderstorm is imminent. However, one Saturday, Tina and I woke earlier than usual to discover a wind-free morning – the perfect day for an outing to Cape Point. I had previously won a prize in a raffle which consisted of free entrance to the nature reserve, breakfast for two, and a return trip in the funicular.

We grasped the opportunity and set off, enjoying the drive along the beautiful coastline. There was little traffic on the roads at that time of the morning. We showed our vouchers at the entrance – the weather was still calm – and drove into the park, towards the Point. We reached the empty parking area – in the next couple of hours, the cars and tour buses would start arriving.

A slight breeze from the south cooled the sun's heat. We headed off to the restaurant for breakfast, where we sat on the deck and soaked up the beauty: everything green from the rains of the past months. As our breakfast arrived, we found ourselves competing for our food with the starlings that perched on the sides of our plates. The waiter had said that the baboons were a menace, hence the electric fencing around the deck, but it was more difficult keeping the birds off the tables!

After our meal, we took the funicular up to the top of the steep hill. We could have walked, but the free tickets made us a little lazy. Once we arrived at the top, we ascended another 200 metres to the lighthouse on concrete stairs that semi-spiralled up the hill. For an unfit person, this would've been quite a strain − even Tina and I had several stops along the way to catch our breath. At the top, we looked around the lighthouse and then went to the wall, peering tentatively over the edge. I have never been one for heights.

In among the rocks, we saw black lizards the length of my hand, of a type I'd never seen before. They are indigenous, but are certainly not found in my garden, and looked almost like miniature crocodiles, their scales seeming to overlap, giving a rough appearance to the skin.

We spent about half an hour up there and then took a slow walk down. We still had much to see in the park. As we got to the bottom, I started to feel queasy.

'This is odd,' I thought, as I was fit − I cycle thirty-five kilometres three times a week. 'Was it the breakfast?'

But Tina was feeling fine. As we took the funicular down to the car park, I started to shiver. Something had to be up − the temperature was thirty degrees out. At the car I pulled on a fleece top, but by the time we had driven about two kilometres, I was shaking like a leaf. We stopped at a few rock pools on the way out, hoping my queasiness would pass, but it only became worse. Tina had to drive us home.

Once there, I went straight to bed, pulling the duvet over

me. But I was still cold, so Tina brought me an extra blanket. I had also developed a headache, a numb ache that turned into a throbbing pain. No stars and floaters appeared before my eyes, yet it was pretty close to a migraine. Strong painkillers brought no relief.

In the early evening, Tina took me to the local Medi-Clinic. Time passes slowly when you are in a waiting room and in pain. Finally, my turn came. The doctor examined me and mentioned that it might be some type of flu virus that was affecting my lungs. He gave me an injection to knock me out – the flu just had to run its course. I was booked off for the next two days.

Back home, I slept until the early hours. Then the vomiting started – as if everything I had ever eaten was coming out of me. I struggle to understand how anyone would want to suffer from bulimia; vomiting is such an unpleasant thing. I finally fell into a deep sleep.

Sunday was a lazy day – the effects of the injection and the painkillers had zonked me out. I dozed and watched cricket on the box. On Monday, as I settled down on the couch to watch a DVD, I felt a stitch-like pain in my right shoulder. It shifted over to my shoulder blade and then the front part of my chest. I struggled to breathe, but managed to call my doctor and tell her about my weekend woes. She urged me to go to the hospital's emergency rooms and ask to see the cardiologist. My neighbour drove me there.

The nurses put me on a bed, attached some plugs to me, checked my heart and set up a drip. They also took blood samples, and the doctor asked question after question. Eventually, I dozed off. Then the doctor returned with the blood test results.

'I'd like the cardiologist to examine you,' he said.

I was X-rayed first, and then admitted into a general ward. Ironically, it was the same ward my mother had been in the year before. By late afternoon, the cardiologist arrived.

'I need you to run on a treadmill so that we can test your heart,' he said. The porter took me to the cardiologist's room in a wheelchair. There, he put me on the treadmill, saying, 'Run for five minutes.'

All the blood tests had been inconclusive, he reported after I finished running. Everything they had tested fell well below the average rate. It was then that he mentioned seeing a haematologist. He didn't believe my problem was my heart, but thought it had more to do with my blood. The porter collected me and I was taken for more blood tests, then back to the ward.

When the haemotologist arrived, I gave him a brief medical history and told him about the blood clots.

'I suspect it might be a blood clot in the left lung,' he said, and asked about childhood illnesses and whether I had ever had tuberculosis. 'TB often causes "scarring" in the lung,' he explained.

I recalled that, at the age of ten, I had been tested for TB, but that the tests had come back negative.

I desperately wanted to go home. The next morning I woke up at the crack of dawn. Hospitals have a habit of waking one at sparrow fart. The cardiologist arrived early and said that I could go home if the haematologist was happy.

'Come to my rooms before leaving,' he said.

I showered and headed for the doctors' rooms. There, he said that was happy with the second batch of tests. But I had to make one sacrifice: 'Stop smoking,' I was told.

I'd had thirty years of cigarettes and, later, flavoured mini-cigars. The doctor was also concerned about the 'thickness' of my blood.

'Take an aspirin every day until everything corrects itself,' he instructed me.

I had to go for a check-up after two weeks. Normal. I had read an article on the risk of vein-related diseases in men with Klinefelter's syndrome. The specialist felt that it was unrelated.

In April 2008, Tina and I went to Wales for a short holiday. On the third day, I noticed lumps the size of a match head on a vein on the side of my penis. A year previously, I had had a similar occurrence. On checking it out with the urologist, and again with the haematologist, I had been told not to worry – the lumps would disappear within a couple of days. (I am unsure whether the doctors knew what had caused them.)

I was not very concerned, but a week later, after returning from our holiday, the lumps were still there. Another trip to the urologist: another round of blood tests. As the nurse inserted the needle and started to draw the blood, the blood began to clot. This, she said, was the first time she'd seen something like this happen; she had to insert another needle.

The results of the test? High cholesterol. Another week elapsed, and still the lumps hadn't gone. The doctor put me on a course of Clexane – an intravenous blood thinner. Unhappy with the slow process, I decided to surf the Net to try to find my own answers.

A website dedicated to blood clots gave no joy. But another site mentioned Mondor's disease – a disease I had never heard of. As I've always been interested in medical matters and am naturally inquisitive, I read on. Bingo! The symptoms resembled mine, and an aspirin a day was recommended as a blood-thinning method. Having taken an aspirin a day for many years, besides the Clexane, I decided to increase the aspirin dosage to twice daily. Eventually the lumps started breaking down quite dramatically and, finally, disappeared.

My urologist had never heard of Mondor's disease and the haematologist was not very concerned about the lumps. But I wondered, 'Is the disease aggravated by the monthly intake of testosterone?'

Well, half a century of my life has come to an end. An end? Perhaps it is only the beginning of my journey, with many joys and tribulations still to come. I can say some of the lessons I've learnt have been for the best. Others have been plain scary.

How did my body celebrate the half a century? At close to fifty, I lost my last two milk teeth. Nothing has replaced them; I am the metal man with a plate in my mouth. Due to the osteoporosis, titanium tooth implants may not be an option, as the bone in my jaw may have insufficient density.

28

Ongoing symptoms

Here I am at fifty-one – the Klinefelter's Kid. Tina and I have been together for two-and-a-half years. Besides dealing with the syndrome and daily life, we also each had a second parent pass away. Nobody said life was going to be easy. Tina has become part of this book and has encouraged the process. The three of us live together – Tina, Klinefelter's and Stephen, the X-rated kid who wanted to be a vet. The neighbour's ginger cat, the fourth member of our family, visits regularly. It obviously knows my needs.

Klinefelter's syndrome has made me a stronger and better person, yet I feel that there is a constant battle going on inside me. Not a moment goes by that I do not wish that I was as normal as everybody else. I am still petrified of studying or learning anything new, as it is such a battle to absorb the information. My memory turns into a ball of shit – I am constantly struggling with myself.

Having said that, I *have* learnt a lot, but I want to learn so much more. At times, I struggle to get the words out. I know that I have the right answers in my head, but, as I am speaking, they all come out wrong. This upsets many people around me. I often fall out of favour with people – even friends. It's like my wires are completely crossed. The blood-clotting problem is ongoing, and nobody out there seems to know what causes it. Once, when I went to see my GP for flu, she asked me how I was and I told her about the blood-clotting. She asked to see the results of the tests that had been done. I also mentioned the funny sensation I have in the left of my chest, in line with the nipple. Every so often I get an ice-cold feeling there, like somebody has put ice blocks inside me, and I feel exhausted for about thirty seconds.

It happened once when I was cycling. I was riding up a hill and suddenly a coldness and extreme exhaustion overcame me. A couple of seconds later I was fine. The sensation has occurred since the time I was hospitalised a year before for a suspected blood clot in the lung.

I got the results and handed them to my doctor. She seemed concerned and referred me to an endocrinologist, whom I was only able to see after a three-month wait. She looked at the blood tests and said that it was possible that I had diabetes; I would have to undergo a glucose test. Klinefelter's syndrome exacerbates the symptoms of diseases, which is an ongoing issue in my life. All those years ago, I had thought that the worst part of the syndrome was not being able to father children – only because I was unaware that I would be diagnosed with osteoporosis at the age of thirty-eight.

Living with Klinefelter's is a continuous battle – one that never ends. I just wait to see what will come up next. It could be diabetes – I know I shouldn't be too shocked, since that is what caused my mother's death. Of course I would be quite upset by this, as my life has not exactly been full of joy. Sometimes I think that enough is enough, but I suppose that each hurdle is just another challenge; I'm sure there will be many more before the day is over.

While I think of the trials and tribulations I've endured, I also reflect on all the learning and positive experiences I've had.

I have come to know who I am and to reach a deep understanding of life and of spirituality. I may never have had these insights without the trials I've endured. One of the biggest experiences that steered me in a different direction was the near-death experience in the Mini. That incident led me to encounter myself in a way I could not have done without it. Somebody was trying to tell me something; perhaps the message was coming directly from the Divine intelligence – God.

I was never a very religious person, but some strange experiences led me to change my point of view. I've learnt to be open to life and what it has in store for me, and that I am an ordinary person with an extra x. But I can be extraordinary in the way I meet my challenges. I've tried to accept myself the way I am; accept the things I can't change and open myself up to unconditional love. Tina came into my life just at the right time. We are there for each other.

When I decided to start writing about my life, I didn't even have a computer. Two friends donated an old one to me, not knowing how long it would last. Eventually the thing conked out, but by then I'd written a fair amount. I met with my editor when I'd written a few thousand words, and she told me that the book still needed a lot of work. So I decided to invest in a new laptop. With no idea how to set up the email facility, I approached the local computer shop for advice.

An assistant in his mid-twenties – a little taller than me, but more rounded, with soft facial features – came over to help me. When he saw my email address – 'stephenxxy' – he looked at me oddly, smiled, and said, 'I know what that means.'

'You've got to be kidding!' I said. 'What does it mean?'

He said that 'xxy' was a chromosome disorder. I asked him if he knew somebody who had the syndrome.

'I've got it,' he said. 'I have Klinefelter's syndrome.'

'That's amazing,' I said. 'Do you mind if I ask you a few questions?'

'Depends on what they are ...' He suddenly seemed self-conscious.

'Are you on testosterone?' I asked.

'No, I can't take it. It makes me too aggressive.'

'Did you struggle at school?' I asked again.

'Yes,' he said.

'So did I,' I reassured him. 'Do you have a girlfriend?'

'No,' he said and backed away from the desk, turning as if to retrieve something from a nearby shelf. 'I don't want to talk about it.'

That was the end of the conversation. I added that I was trying to write a book about my experiences with Klinefelter's, but he seemed to have lost interest. I tried to tell him how special people like us are and that he must never worry about what other people think. He helped me with the computer but then said that he needed to get back to work.

What a pity. I wish I could have spoken to him for longer, as I would like to be of help to others with the same problem. But he just seemed to switch off.

I felt a surge of compassion for him, and then I realised it was because I had once been that boy: it was like looking at me when I was about the same age. I was standing on the other side of the fence looking at the shy, introverted person I used to be; the chap with the boyish features. I started to understand a little more about myself and realised how I, too, would just switch off and retreat into my own little world at times. Writing this book has helped me reach back to the boy I once was and, in so doing, heal the man I am now.

What is Klinefelter's syndrome?

In 1942, Dr Harry Klinefelter, while working in a general hospital in Boston, together with other researchers, published a report about nine male individuals with similar features, including enlarged breasts and sparse facial and body hair. By the late 1950s, researchers found that these males had an extra x chromosome in most of their cells, and were xxy instead of the typical male xy. They discovered that the egg splits in the womb in a similar process to that of Down's syndrome, retaining an extra chromosome on the sex gene. It is unknown why this occurs, but research continues and, hopefully, the reason will be found.

Not every xxy male has all the symptoms of Klinefelter's, even though all men with the syndrome have the extra x chromosome. The terms 'xxy male' or 'xxy' are thus commonly used to describe the condition.

The xxy condition can affect three main areas of development:

Physical development: As babies, many xxy males have weak muscles and reduced strength. Their development is slower than that of other infants. After about age four, xxy males tend to be taller and may have less muscle control than other boys their age.

As xxy males enter puberty, their bodies often don't produce as much testosterone as other boys. This can lead to a taller, less muscular body, sparser facial and body hair, and broader hips than other boys. As teens, xxy males may have larger breasts, weaker bones and a lower level of energy than their peers.

By adulthood, xxy males look similar to males without the condition, although they are often taller. They are also more likely than other men to develop certain health problems, such as autoimmune disorders, breast cancer, vein diseases, osteoporosis and tooth decay.

Although xxy males can have normal sex lives, between 95 per cent and 99 per cent are infertile because their bodies produce insufficient sperm.

Language development: As boys, between 25 per cent and 85 per cent of xxy males have language problems of some kind, such as learning to talk late; trouble using language to express thoughts and needs; problems reading; and trouble processing what they hear.

As adults, they may have a harder time doing work that involves reading and writing, but most hold down jobs and have successful careers.

Social development: As babies, xxy males tend to be quiet and undemanding. As they get older, they are usually quieter, less self-confident, less active, and more helpful and obedient than other boys.

As teens, xxy males tend to be quiet and shy. They may struggle in school and sports, meaning they may have trouble 'fitting in' with other kids. However, as adults, xxy males live

lives similar to men without the condition; they have friends, families and normal social relationships.
(Adapted from www.medicenet.com)

Klinefelter's syndrome seems to have come to the fore in South Africa only in the 1970s. The syndrome only occurs in males. Statistics say 1 in 500, but the prevalence is probably more likely 1 in 1 000. The numbers increase as more knowledge about the syndrome is gained and recognised.

The characteristics include:

- Tallness and lankiness
  (usually around six foot or 1.83 metres)
- Sparse facial and body hair
- Small testicles, hence the inability to produce sperm – therefore sterility
- Decreased libido
- Osteoporosis
- Taurodontism – exposure of nerves due to thinner enamel on the teeth
- Venous diseases
- Autoimmune disorders
- Low energy
- Low self-esteem, exacerbating the introverted and shy nature
- Communication difficulties, especially in expressive language
- Frustration-based outbursts
- Learning, emotional and mental disorders
- Developmental delays
- Problems with motor skills
- Gynaecomastia – the enlargement of the breasts

I can tick off most of this list, as well as items not on it too. For instance, I got my first teeth only at thirteen months. When my mother asked her doctor about this, he just laughed and said, 'There's nothing to worry about. Some children are late starters.'

I was to live with these milk teeth for a long time.

From Christine

Stephen is my younger brother by eighteen months. My first recollection is of a little boy dragging a blanket of sorts, sucking his thumb, looking out through these thick Coke-bottle prescription glasses. His eyes seemed to peer over the top – sad, vulnerable, glassy-green eyes. I guess he was about three at the time.

My mother maintained I always looked out for Stephen because she worked all day and night. I don't actually recall that. I do remember being distraught that I never had a mother around. She worked during the day, and also six nights a week at the local cinema. I was more involved in my own emptiness than anyone else's. However, our mom said I was always protecting Stephen while mothering him. Perhaps I just *did* it?

Stephen had a couple of good friends in the neighbourhood and seemed to get on fine with his daily life. Although I do remember that he struggled through school and was held back a couple of times. In those days, the schools weren't really interested in social issues, thus they would merely inform the family that he had failed! Here was a youngster who needed extra lessons and perhaps one-on-one teaching, but it hadn't even been a remote possibility at the time.

My parents were struggling to keep food on the table and

Stephen's not coping was a small issue in comparison. It must be said that Stephen is by no means lacking in intelligence! On the contrary, he can be extremely astute and perceptive.

As Stephen ventured into his teenage years, he always looked extremely young for his age, and was also emotionally immature. I had become involved with a friend who was a typical 'macho' sports guy and wasn't scared to pick a fight – the antithesis of Stephen. Our older brother Johnny was also extremely sporty and stayed out of the house as often as he could. In hindsight, I suppose he was trying to get away from his pain.

Stephen was less successful and fraught with complexes and insecurities. Did he have no means of escaping? These 'macho' guys around him probably aggravated his insecurities in a world that recognises testosterone in males. It was not a time when alternative views were sought. You conformed or you simply did not fit in!

I think back and wonder when Stephen became aware that he was different. I could see it later in my life, but while living with him, I did not put my finger on it. He always had some type of illness, break, cut or bruise. It was not because he was boisterous in any way; on the contrary, he was not physically active at all. He was certainly more accident-prone than was regarded as normal, but I think he also desperately needed some attention. We had a home, but – God bless my parents – a home that simply had no time to love and pay attention to anyone.

Our mom was exhausted for the nine years she worked both day and night. To further exacerbate this, she was constantly trying to make ends meet. She also had a husband who was mentally handicapped and unable to assist in any child rearing, finance, or in any other way, other than being company when he was able to be coherent.

I know I suffered from a huge lack of attention, and I latched on to my mother to force her to pay me that much-needed notice. I met her at the bus stop every night after she came home from her office job. I would sit with her while she prepared dinner, and I would walk again with her to the bus stop if it was still light. I also waited for her to come home each night so I could see her, although when she worked until midnight I had little chance of that and would fall into bed, scared, tired and alone. I forced myself into the little bit of space she had left. Stephen hung back and seemed to be in the shadows.

I don't recall much of either of my brothers at this time, as I was probably only trying to survive myself. I escaped into books and read from a very young age. Where was Stephen during these tumultuous years? Was he peripheral and lounging about the house somewhere? Heaven knows, it was a minute box of a house − one could hardly get lost! − but I don't remember him or Johnny at that time. Was I too woeful to contemplate others?

Going back to Steve's sicknesses and ailments − I am certain that he was truly medically less healthy than most people, but I also think he may have had an unconscious desire to attract some sort of attention. How could he not have? Don't we do what we have to do to survive? Mom was always interested in medical matters − the area in which she paid us the most notice. She also often mentioned how much bad luck Stephen endured. She spoke sadly of his awful bad fortune. Did this instil in him a learnt helplessness?

Stephen *was* different, and yet he was not embraced for that difference. It was rather like a cloak of darkness that seemed to shroud him. He needed to be protected and nurtured, while being praised for his differences, but unfortunately there was no one who understood or had the time to cultivate him. Today he would perhaps have been commended for his difference.

I think that Stephen developed his insecurity or lack of self-worth predominantly because no one afforded him any consideration. His inability to fend for himself made him lash out, made him angry and unable to converse. He loves talking, but I sometimes think he isn't able to listen. He has a lot to offer regarding many subjects, and particularly esoteric issues. He can have amazing insight on one occasion, but can seem totally oblivious to someone's plight on another.

Steve's inability to make himself understood is, I think, at the core of many of his frustrations. He does not seem to be able to articulate his thoughts in the manner in which he would like to; thus people misread him. I also believe his inability to hear others results in people eventually giving up on and discarding him. I think this sometimes makes him defensive and leads to deep disappointment. However, even when one attempts to explain, one has the sense that he is not listening or taking in what you are saying. He can be quite dogmatic and stubborn, which, in this case, exacerbates his defensiveness.

Sometimes I think Stephen lacks social etiquette and that he is totally unaware that he may be offending people. It gets people's backs up and then he, quite rightly, picks up on their antagonism. Yet he is unable to see where it came from. He seems almost oblivious to social niceties and seems to take everything for granted. I do not believe he has any idea that he does this. Of course, it is offensive to people and, once again, he comes under attack. He is extremely sensitive and easily offended – even when things are not necessarily directed at him personally. He almost always finds someone in the room who has snubbed him, thus making enemies before he has even begun.

I think his lack of insight has made life extremely difficult for him. He is all about energies, but perhaps he does not realise that his are so often negative and out of sync. He can be oblivious to people's discomfort and to social 'hints'. It's as though he is missing the cues. Does he need to listen more; to receive more and to stop transmitting? He has pertinent points to contribute and is interesting and attractive, but can be too serious and heavy at times. He should laugh more and criticise less; he has a lovely smile and a terrific sense of humour when he lets himself go.

My cousin Colleen made an accurate observation about Stephen, which my husband Raymond also acknowledged – Steve is very determined and tenacious. Colleen said that when she dealt with him in business he was extremely ethical and went the 'extra mile'. He never gave up and persisted until a task was completed. He perseveres when he wants something badly enough.

Our mom used to love her chats with Stephen and often said how interesting he was, but he could also send her spiralling into frustration because he could not see beyond his own point of view.

Be that as it may, Stephen's good qualities far outweigh his bad ones. And who's to judge, anyway? Stephen is scrupulously honest, direct and forthright. He has integrity and high values and principles. He always tries to do the right thing – and indeed this has landed him in a lot of hot water at times. He is unable to stand by and let unfairness or unjustness prevail and has an overwhelming sense of right and wrong. He is kind and gentle and has a deep love of animals.

I think a lot of Stephen's hurts and anxieties are interwoven with his feelings of being misunderstood. He has good intentions and motivations and yet there always seem to be stumbling blocks in his way – not merely challenges, but insurmountable obstacles. He then battles to articulate his feelings and even his intentions and the messages become muddled and misunderstood. It must be exhausting and frustrating beyond belief. So much of the confusion is, I believe, over his inability to express himself successfully, thus leading people to get the wrong impression. I can't help seeing a picture of an individual speaking Japanese, trying to communicate with a person who is only able to speak Greek. Some messages are clear; however, the bulk of the conversation goes uncomprehended. The nuances and subtleties are missed. How exhausting, how trying!

This is an extremely difficult analysis to write, as it seems critical and arrogant. Which one of us is perfect, or even anywhere near perfection? I have many faults – I am pushy and bold and force my point across – so it seems presumptuous even to mention Stephen's. However, for the purposes of his book, I have attempted to reflect my reality as closely as I can.

Stevie – you go, boy! I believe in you and am convinced that Lady Luck will smile upon you because you have tried so hard and fought such a battle.

May God bless you always, my friend, my brother!

From Tina

How best to describe living with Stephen? Wonderful and infuriating. When I first met Stephen, I was immediately attracted to him. Does anyone ever know why they are attracted to another? As our relationship progressed, I began to get irritated with him (I am not the most patient person). I could not get to grips with the way he thought and expressed himself. At times the conversation was difficult. He explained things in a very roundabout way – he never seemed to get to the point.

There were times when I thought he was stupid. I worried about what he might say in front of my friends, and in return what they would then think of me – choosing a dumb guy. The irritation got to a point of no return. I ended our time together.

After about two months, I realised I missed the 'boy'. The lightness was missing from my life. We got back together and – although it was a trying time, with his mother in hospital – I realised that this man, with his childish pranks and bad English, brought immense joy to me. And did the language really matter? I just had to stop my tendency to correct his English – something everybody around him has done for most of his life.

But time has moved on, and I realise and accept that Stephen is the eternal child. He never knows when it is appropriate to act the adult. In a serious discussion, he will make jokes, giving me the impression that the matter is of no importance to him. I know most of us take life too seriously, but Stephen tries to make light of any trauma. Deep down I know that he really does care and has sincere empathy.

It is difficult to remain cross with Stephen for any length of time. He plays harmless, practical jokes to lighten the mood.

But these can also be annoying – as he doesn't know the meaning of 'enough already'.

He has the biggest heart, but if you need him to listen, you actually have to hold his hands to keep his attention. Halfway through a discussion, the birds outside will catch his eye and, no matter how pressing the situation, you have lost him. Patience is what I am learning in this relationship.

Many things have to be explained more than once – tasks that seem so simple to understand. You begin to feel that you are at fault for not explaining properly. He also battles to express himself and becomes angry when I cannot understand him. Stephen has an extreme temper, I think mainly due to his frustrations at being misunderstood. Having read the 'baby journal', I see that this has been an ongoing pattern.

During a discussion, he may suddenly change tack, expecting you to know exactly what is going on inside his head. I often tell him that his head works faster than his mouth. My inability to keep up also irritates him and has caused many an argument.

Stephen cannot be interrupted while telling a story: he loses the gist. You have to wait until the end to ask any relevant questions or again the frustration surfaces and nine times out of ten, he will not finish the tale.

He is like a jack-in-the-box; he cannot sit still. When he is restless, he looks in cupboards as though a 'task' will appear. He also has to do chores *now*. I know this can be seen as a positive, but it can also be rather annoying, especially when a good movie has just started on the box.

Stephen becomes very tired at times – usually close to his

jab time. I am still trying to establish just how much his mood changes at these times.

Although his ailments continue – I have accused him of being a hypochondriac – he manages to take it all in his stride.

Stephen prefers the company of females. He does not relate well to 'macho' men. No, he doesn't enjoy rugby. Please understand – it does not mean that he is in any way effeminate; purely that his sensitive side is more developed. The esoteric would call him an evolved man, one who relates better to women than men, in touch with his own feelings and those of others. Sometimes I think Stephen is more of a girl than I am – he cannot pass the perfume counter without a spray! He makes a point of buying good eau de cologne.

Stephen is accepting of the meek, helping any lost soul (including animals). His sensitivity and trust of others leave him wide open to abuse. Some have taken advantage of this and he has felt that hurt – deeply.

Although Stephen's honesty is refreshing, I am sure it must upset people too. His bluntness – together with his language weakness – does not help him to make friends; rather, it alienates people.

Stephen has suffered many setbacks and yet continues to move forward – ever positive. After reading the 'analysis' from me and Christine, he is more surprised than hurt. He praises our honesty.

To end, I would like to say – *Stephen is not stupid*. He can hold his own. In fact, most people really enjoy his conversation – wrong words and all!

Having helped him with this book, I have a far more intimate knowledge of many aspects of him, including his dark side.

Without this insight, and the understanding of his downfalls, perhaps I would have given up on the relationship again. That would be my loss.

Love you.

Klinefelter's syndrome

http://47xxy.org/PrintXXY.htm

http://www.aafp.org/afp/20051201/2259.html

http://care.diabetesjournal.org/cgi/content/abstract/29/7/1591

http://www.emedicine.com/ped/topic1252.htm

http://www.fightingmaster.com

http://ghr.nlm.nih.gov/handbook/mutationsanddisorders/
chromosomalconditions

http://www.klinefelter.org.uk/whatisKS.htm

http://www.medicinenet.com/klinefelter_syndrome/page2.htm

The Foster Gang

Clarke, J. *Like it was – The Star 100 Years in Johannesburg.* Johannesburg: The Argus Printing and Publishing Company, 1987.

Joyce, Peter. *South Africa in the Twentieth Century: Chronicles of an Era.* Cape Town: Struik, 2000.

'Public Enemy Number One: The Foster Gang: 1914'. http://www.africacrime-mystery.co.za/books/fsac/chp2.htm: .

'The Foster Gang: Raiders of the Secret Cave'. http://www.joburg.org.za/view/244/51:

With Christine and Dolly

Me and Christine. I was five years old

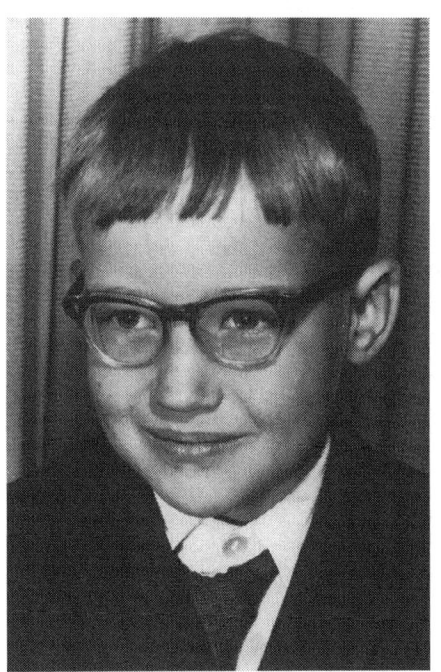

Me, aged eight

Dad, Mom, Christine and me at the house
in Clacton Road, Kensington

With my dog Ringo and a house cat. I must have been about twelve

Luis and me. I was about thirteen or fourteen

At Durban beach. I was fifteen and much smaller than my friends

Me, at the age of about twenty-five, with my mom and dad

In my mid-thirties

Me, today

Made in the USA
Columbia, SC
28 May 2022

61049085R00161